Breeding for Racing

By the same author

Steeplechasing (with John Skeaping)
From Start to Finish
The Turf
Far from a Gentleman
Anything but a Soldier
The Brigadier
Flat Race Riding
Of Horses and Races
Racing Reflections

Breeding For Racing

JOHN HISLOP

The Kingswood Press

First published in Great Britain in 1976
by Martin Secker and Warburg Ltd
Reprinted 1980
This revised edition published 1992
by The Kingswood Press
an imprint of Methuen London
Michelin House, 81 Fulham Road, London sw3 6rb

A CIP catalogue record for this book
is available from the British Library
ISBN 0 413 66470 8

Printed in Great Britain
by Mackays of Chatham Plc

Contents

Illustrations

Acknowledgement for permission to reproduce the photographs is due to John Crofts Photography for plates 1b and 3b; W. W. Rouch & Co. for plates 2a, 2b, 4a, 4b, 4c, 5b, 7a, 8b, 9a, 10b, 11a and 11b; R. Anscomb for plates 3a and 7b; Fiona Vigors for plate 5c; *Daily Express* for plate 6b; Keeneland – Meadors for plate 8a; and Colorlabs International for plate 12a.

Preface to the New Edition

Though the basic principles of Thorough-bred breeding remain unchanged, the shape of the breed does not. In a few years important names recede too far back in pedigrees to be of practical value in the present and new influences make themselves felt.

Experience points to revision of old ideas, and changes in racing programmes are reflected in the type of racehorse being produced. These aspects are considered in this new edition, as a result of which Chapter 8, 'Important Names in the Modern Thoroughbred', has been completely rewritten, and the rest of the book revised and updated where necessary.

John Hislop
1992

Introduction

Breeding racehorses is an inexact science; there are certain principles which are a help to success, but they neither ensure it nor provide a guarantee against failure. In the long run, given similar material, the breeder who works on sound lines will do better than the one who does not. Likewise, though good horses have sometimes been bred in the most adverse circumstances, continued use of bad methods will lead to disaster sooner or later.

As in the human race, it is almost impossible to keep a true champion down. He will rise above everything – bad breeding methods, bad training and bad riding. The most may not be made of him, but it will be impossible to hide his brilliance. Champions, however, are few and far between, and the advent of one in face of bad management is no reason to believe that other good performers will be produced by similar methods. In such cases, the credit goes to a fortuitous genetic make-up, not to environment and upbringing.

To determine whether he is on the right lines, or not, a breeder must examine his results in the light of opportunity and not merely on bare figures. If, with good mares and the use of good stallions, his results consistently fall below expectations, there is something wrong with his methods and unless the fault is detected and eradicated, consistent disappointment will result.

A principle to be grasped is that between racing and breeding for sale there is a great gulf; the two departments bear almost no relation to each other. Therefore it is imperative that a breeder should make up his mind exactly what path he is to take; otherwise he will end in a jungle of confusion. Breeding for sale in England, unless it can be merged into another operation such as farming or running a large estate, is at present severely penalised by taxation, particularly VAT. The breeder here has no chance whatever against his opposite number in the Republic of Ireland, whose far more favourable terms of

taxation (at least up to the time of writing) give him immeasur-
ably greater scope in the use of stallions and the general
financial conduct of his stud, compared with his English counterpart. The chief worry of Irish commercial breeders is that
below top international level the market is contracting and
buyers disappearing. Thus, quality must be given precedence
over quantity.

While this book is addressed to the breeder who races his own
stock, it is pertinent to consider briefly the aspect of breeding
for sale, so that the difference between the two schools can be
appreciated.

The breeder who races his own stock has only one aim: to
establish a stud which consistently produces good, sound racehorses. He has only himself to please. The commercial breeder's
target is to put on the market yearlings which will show a
profit. Strangely enough, as the results of the yearling sales will
show, breeding winners is not necessarily related to obtaining
high prices for yearlings. To obtain a high price for a yearling
the latter must be well grown, look sleek and big in condition,
be handsome, have a fashionable stallion as a sire and appear
likely to win as a two-year-old or have a pedigree indicating
classic possibilities. Even a yearling who is out of the dam of a
good winner does not always make a high price if he is either by
a sire who is out of fashion or does not take the eye as an
individual. Buyers get tired of sires who have been around for a
number of years, despite their having got successful horses in
the past. As a result, yearlings by such sires often do not make
as much as they deserve to do. An instance is Authi, a winner
in high-class company and placed in top races in France, who
made the comparatively modest price of 14,500 guineas as a
yearling in 1971, though a son of the proven classic sire Aureole
out of the dam of the French Derby winner Hard to Beat, a son
of the rather unfashionable Hardicanute. Hard to Beat cost only
920 guineas as a yearling and, like his half-brother, was bred by
the Tally-Ho Stud in Ireland. This is a typical example of the
fate of commercial yearlings bred on non-commercial lines and
a case of virtue going meagrely rewarded. In France, commercial
breeders are safeguarded against receiving no compensation for
a yearling cheaply sold who turns out to be a good racehorse, by
breeders' premiums through which a breeder receives a percent-

age of the prize. In England there is no money available for such luxuries.

As a result of the attitude of governments in England, which seems unlikely to change, breeding yearlings for sale is a poor proposition. Those embarking on it are advised to do so with their eyes wide open, especially if the operation is not linked with some other lucrative venture.

Commercial breeders with high ambitions must aim to attract the big buyers in the international market, who are only interested in the stock of the most fashionable stallions and of good mares. The Americans, especially, rate performance on the racecourse very highly and for them to give a substantial price a yearling must have everything. Certainly, big prices are sometimes obtained for yearlings with flaws, either of conformation, pedigree or racing and breeding performance in the tail-female line; but such exceptions are usually due to the whims of individual buyers, alcoholic euphoria or the desire to outbid a rival buyer. While all goes well for a commercial breeder operating on this level the money will come rolling in, but a run of bad luck, an error of judgement or a slump in the bloodstock market can cause financial crisis which only a rich man can survive.

As I learnt in the hard school of experience, breeding middle-distance horses below the top class for sale as yearlings is the path to penury. No one wants them at anything but a knock-down price, and should they turn out any good, the breeder has only been working for someone else's benefit. This is a disheartening and unrewarding operation. When breeding yearlings for sale in partnership with the late Patrick Dennis, we produced a fine-looking colt by Mieuxce out of Brazen Molly, the eventual grandam of Brigadier Gerard. Mieuxce had won the French Derby and the Grand Prix de Paris, was imported to England by the late Sir Victor Sassoon at the end of the horse's three-year-old career and did fairly well as a sire, though his only classic winner in England was Commotion, successful in the Oaks during the war. Not surprisingly, buyers of yearlings in general were not interested in our colt, despite his good looks, and but for Sir Victor Sassoon being attracted by him because he owned his sire, he would have gone to Peter Thrale – an astute judge who was entirely uninfluenced by fashion – for a pittance. As it was, he made 2,000 guineas in 1949, which showed just a fair profit. Named Stokes, the colt won the Spring Stakes at Newmarket, the Windsor Castle Stakes at Royal Ascot and finished second in the Two Thousand Guineas. Had we kept him and raced him ourselves, we would have made a great deal of money out of him, tax free. This experience helped to cure me of commercial breeding and I can imagine, with sympathy, the feeling of the Holland-Martins when Grundy, whom they bred at their Overbury Stud and sold for 11,000 guineas in 1973, won a fortune in stakes and was sold for over a million. Admittedly, the breeder who races his own horses cannot afford to make many mistakes, but he does stand a chance of hitting the jackpot, which the commercial breeder under the yoke of English taxation never does.

I would rate the late George Harris of Ballykisteen Stud, Co. Tipperary, as about the most successful commercial breeder of my time. In the first place, he never gave high prices for mares or stallions, yet had an unerring knack of buying good ones. He was not over-ambitious, in that he confined himself to breeding the type of yearling the average buyer wanted, as opposed to prospective classic horses. Thus, assisted by the use of his own stallions, he was able to put into the ring yearlings which did not have to make unduly high prices to show a profit. Though prospective two-year-olds were his main objective, he sometimes produced horses well above ordinary commercial standards, notably the One Thousand Guineas winner Happy Laughter. One principle to which he always kept was that of choosing mares tracing to really good tap-roots; these read well in the catalogue. His purchase of stallions was especially astute, as evident in such as Denturius, The Phoenix, Pall Mall and Will Somers. He once told me that after the failure his father experienced with the stayer Santoi, no long-distance horses were ever again bought for the Ballykisteen Stud. Needless to say, the yearlings were always extremely well produced and no misfits were ever sent to Newmarket to spoil the image of the stud. It is important for commercial breeders to send a level lot up for sale. If a vendor's yearlings differ widely in type and size, the draft has a ragged appearance and the eye of buyers is thrown out: the big yearlings look too big and the small ones too small.

There is no rule-of-thumb way in which a commercial breeder can emulate George Harris, because so much depends upon personal flair. This was particularly marked in his ability to pick out horses that turned out to be successful stallions, a feat which entails a 'crystal-ball' sense. Of all matters of judgement in breeding, that of foretelling whether a horse is or is not going to make a good stallion is the most unpredictable.

In the present situation, probably the best advice to the average commercial breeder in England is to aim to produce yearlings which will show a reasonable profit, rather than aim at top prices. This entails sound judgement in buying mares and in the use of stallions. The chief aim should be: good looks, speed, the use of stallions in fashion and a level draft well conditioned and turned out.

The late Michael Beary once told me that a very successful Irish commercial breeder of the past, when wanting to find a prospective broodmare, tried to buy the best two-year-old filly on the market. Provided her make and shape is right, this is not a bad principle on which to work, as such a mare should stand a good chance of breeding the type of yearling which the average buyer is seeking. He need not be too choosy about pedigree, so long as she is not a fluke in that there are no other winners of merit in the early removes of the tail-female line, because many buyers do not look much further than the sire of a yearling and the record of the dam at stud and on the racecourse. Sometimes an oldish mare is quite a good proposition if she has already proved she can breed yearlings who attract buyers. The reason is that buyers of good mares will only give high prices for fairly young mares, and a breeder who is willing to take a chance on an old mare, even if it means getting only one or a couple of foals out of her, can buy her cheaply and perhaps show a good profit. Many years ago I bought a sweet fifteen-year-old mare for Pat Dennis called Rainbow (Obliterate–Carina, by Chaucer) who cost only 50 guineas. She had bred two or three winners and was in foal to Holywell (Blandford–Double Life, dam of Precipitation and Persian Gulf), an unfashionable sire who never raced and did little at stud. She produced two good foals, each of whom made over 700 guineas and subsequently won.

The choice of stallions is extremely difficult for the commercial breeder, since fashion changes as quickly and unpredictably as it does in women's clothes. One safe bet is to use a first-season sire of the right type since buyers are always on the look-out for something new. The stallion is then discarded and a new first-season horse patronized. The breeder can then wait to see how the stock of the first stallion fares and, if desirable, return to him, even if it means paying an increased fee. If he is lucky enough to own or have shares in a stallion who comes up trumps, the breeder is set fair for a number of years; otherwise he has to think hard, judge well and be lucky.

It is sometimes possible to buy a share in a youngish stallion who has shown that he can sire good horses but is temporarily out of fashion, perhaps because of a couple of lean years. This can happen to any stallion and may not be his fault: promising stock by him may meet with an accident, go abroad, die or be badly trained or managed. Thus for two breeders I was able to buy in one case a share in Crepello and in the other a share in Derring-Do, after both had proved able to sire good horses, for sums which a couple of years later were exceeded by the price of nominations to them when they returned to fashion.

Always the commercial breeder must have in mind value for money, allied with putting into the ring the stamp of yearling which buyers want, at a reasonable profit for the breeder. It is pointless to obtain 8,000 guineas for a lot if it cost 10,000 guineas to produce. On the other hand, 8,000 guineas for one which cost 5,000 guineas to put into the ring is a business proposition.

There is no school like that of experience, particularly when the individual concerned is risking his own money and does not have a great deal of it. Had I known what I was about when starting as a commercial breeder, and followed the precepts quoted above, I would have saved myself thousands of pounds.

Whether a breeder chooses to operate commercially or privately is a matter of personal philosophy. The most successful commercial breeders I have known find more pleasure in seeing a really well-produced draft of yearlings make top prices than in having their colours carried to victory on the racecourse. For them the winning post is the sale-ring; anything that happens after that is of secondary interest, even if it entails one of their products winning the Derby. Commercial breeding is an art in itself, requiring horsemastership, showmanship and salesmanship, the latter two qualities often lacking in the private breeder. All this must be backed by good stud management, a first-class staff and close personal attention to detail.

While certain factors are common both to commercial breeding and breeding for racing, such as good staff and sound stud management, the philosophy of the private breeder is by the nature of the enterprise quite different from that of his commercial counterpart.

If the private breeder sets out with the primary object of making money, he will never be able to get the best out of his stud and may even ruin it by selling good mares and fillies, which has happened in more than one case.

His philosophy must be to try to breed good horses without going broke in the process. If he succeeds, the money will follow; but if he lets commercialism take charge he is doomed as regards reaching the top as a private breeder.

Inevitably, a private breeder will have to sell mares and fillies to avoid becoming overstocked and, inevitably, he may sell one who will breed a good horse for someone else. This possibility cannot be avoided because breeding is largely unpredictable and a change of environment can sometimes produce results which would not have been possible if the mare or filly in question had remained at home. The risk is a fact of life in the world of racing and breeding, however unpalatable, and must be accepted.

The bitterness of a paramount ambition dashed by the sale of a horse has never been illustrated more poignantly than when Lord George Bentinck sold all his bloodstock to devote himself to Parliament, and Surplice, whom he had bred and who was one of the horses in the sale, won the Derby.

The description of Disraeli's meeting with Bentinck in the House of Commons after Surplice's victory bears repetition.

He was standing before the bookshelves with a volume in his hand, and his countenance was greatly disturbed. His resolutions in favour of the Colonial interest, after all his labours, had been negatived by the Committee on the 22nd; on the 24th, the horse Surplice, whom he had parted with among the rest of his stud, solely that he might pursue without distraction his labours on behalf of the great interests of the country, had won that paramount and Olympic stake to gain which had been the object of his life. He had nothing to console him and nothing to sustain him, except his pride. Even that deserted him before a heart which he knew at least could yield him sympathy. He gave a sort of superb groan.

'All my life I have been trying for this, and for what have I sacrificed it?' he murmured. It was vain to offer solace. 'You do not know what the Derby is,' he moaned.

'Yes, I do, it is the *Blue Riband of the Turf*.'

'It *is* the Blue Riband of the Turf,' he slowly repeated; and sitting down at a table, buried himself in a folio of statistics.

No dedicated owner-breeder can fail to be moved by Bentinck's sentiments, the more so as he sold the horse from altruistic motives, knowing what the outcome might be. And as I stood in the winner's enclosure watching Brigadier Gerard being unsaddled after his victory in the Two Thousand Guineas I thought of Lord George Bentinck and Surplice, and I realized that if the Brigadier had won in any other colours it would have broken my heart, as the victory of Surplice in the Derby broke Bentinck's.

To be forced by circumstances to sell a future Derby winner, who otherwise would have been raced by his owner, as was the case with Surplice, is a bitter pill compared with the success of a horse culled because he did not appear good enough to keep. That is the luck of the game, as opposed to lack of judgement or the sale of a classic prospect through force of circumstance. Moreover, such sales have their consolation, since they encourage buyers to give inflated prices for surplus stock sent up from the stud afterwards. When he sold the dams of Supreme Court, winner of the King George VI and Queen Elizabeth Festival of Britain Stakes, and Premonition, who won the St Leger, the late Lt-Col. Giles Loder so caught the imagination of buyers that any lot from his stud submitted in the years that followed made a huge price. Giles Loder suffered no sharp pangs of regret at the victories of Supreme Court and Premonition, as he had already won the Derby with Spion Kop and the One Thousand Guineas with Cresta Run, as well as many other notable races, so had made his name as an owner-breeder at classic level and had little more to gain in this respect. Had he never bred a horse of the calibre of Supreme Court or Premonition it would have been a different matter. By the same token, if we had sold Brigadier Gerard before he won the Two Thousand, the opportunity of owning such a horse might never have come again. In the world of Thoroughbred breeding, especially in the case of those operating on a modest scale, the postman seldom knocks twice.

Before anyone sets out to breed racehorses, he should realize the implications. It is an expensive enterprise in which consistent success can only be achieved through favourable environment, knowledge, experience, good management, intelligent planning, hard work, good staff, close attention to detail and a measure of luck. Money alone is not enough.

If the breeder does not possess the necessary knowledge and experience, or does not wish to acquire it by the hard, lengthy and costly process of trial and error, he will be well advised to employ a competent manager or adviser. Above all, he must be dedicated and have a clear aim; a muddled policy or no policy at all will lead to chaos. He cannot be both a commercial breeder and a private breeder and if his category is the former he may well find it desirable to close this book now.

Should the breeder decide to press on, I hope that he may find some practical information to his advantage. The subject matter is based on personal trial and error, study and the advice and observation of those who have succeeded as breeders. The tedium of frequent reference to our own horses will, I trust, be excused since they offer wider and more detailed information than those of other people, with whom I am less familiar.

Choosing a Stud

The first step in starting a private stud, apart from having sufficient money to buy it, preferably by legitimate means – as opposed to the owner, no longer in this world, who acquired a subsequent Derby winner and started a stud on fraudulently accumulated wealth, an operation which eventually caught up with him – is to find somewhere to keep the mares.

If a breeder cannot afford to buy or rent an existing stud, this entails making one from scratch or boarding his stock at someone else's stud.

Whatever method is chosen, one essential is common to all three: the land and water-supply must be suitable to producing good racehorses.

The longer I breed racehorses, the more convinced do I become that the land on which horses are raised is a far, far more important factor than is appreciated generally. Mares of the highest class, use of the most successful stallions, the finest feeding and management can all be thwarted if the land and water supply are not suitable.

The best way of determining whether land is suitable for breeding racehorses, or not, is by trial and error, but this is a long process and by the time the answer has been found the breeder may have run out of money or be dead.

The problem is complicated further as outstanding racehorses have been bred in vastly differing environments. Bahram was bred in Ireland, Blue Peter in Buckinghamshire, Nijinsky in Canada, Mill Reef in Virginia, Brigadier Gerard in Berkshire, Tudor Minstrel in Sussex and so on. Nor are scientific tests of land infallible guides: studs have been known to pass these well, but fail to breed winners of a class consistent with the quality of the stock. There are certain negative guides indicating that the land is unlikely to prove ideal for breeding racehorses, such as cold, heavy, exposed land; or pasture admirable for fattening livestock, but too lush for horses; or land with no depth of soil; but it is not easy to lay down hard-and-fast rules.

The most dangerous move is to choose a property on account of the beauty of the house or the surrounding countryside, regardless of the suitability of the land to the purpose. There is little pleasure to the dedicated breeder in looking from his superb Queen Anne house at a delightful vista if the foreground is marred by a group of bad-legged, undersized – or overgrown – common-looking yearlings with nothing to recommend them but their pedigrees and little prospect of their winning more than a maiden race or a seller. However much it may offend the architectural susceptibilities of his spouse or family, he will be a happier and richer man if, turning his back on his hideous Victorian or Edwardian abode, he can gaze with pride at some beautiful foals or yearlings, each looking a real racehorse in the making and difficult to fault by the best show-ring standards.

Thus, in the choice of a stud a breeder should put the suitability of the land before all else, even at the risk of it leading to domestic argument or the very doors of the divorce court, if he hopes to make a success of the enterprise.

Finding a ready-made stud upon which good winners have been bred is probably the safest bet, but care must be taken that it is neither horse-sick nor has been run down by bad management. In this case it will need time and good farming of the pastures to bring it back. If the breeder is prepared to spend the time and money to do this, the eventual result should be satisfactory, since fundamentally the land is good, but if his patience or age makes the delay insupportable he will have to look elsewhere.

This leaves the alternative of finding an existing but unproven stud, forming a completely new one or boarding the stock out.

Deciding upon an existing unproven stud or founding a new one means that the quality and suitability of the land is uncertain. Some guide to the answer may be found if there is a successful stud in the immediate vicinity, situated on similar soil. This was the case when we acquired our own stud at East Woodhay House, near Newbury. It had been founded in the 1930s and used to house two stallions, Hairan (Fairway–Harpsichord, by Louvois) and Rameses II (Gainsborough–Grande Rapide, by Hurry On). Hairan was exported to the USA at an early stage of his stud career, while Rameses II received scant patronage, his chief claim to distinction as a sire being that he got the Cheltenham Gold Cup winner Red Rower.

Thus the stud at that stage had not had a chance to prove whether or not winners could be bred on it. However, close by were the Woolton House Stud and the Harwood Stud (now the Gainsborough Stud), the former having produced Supreme Court (Persian Gulf or Precipitation–Forecourt, by Fair Trial). Other top-class winners to follow included Altesse Royal (Saint Crespin III–Bleu Azur, by Crepello), winner of the One Thousand Guineas, Oaks and Irish Guinness Oaks. The Harwood Stud had earned immortality by having produced the triple crown winner and famous sire, Gainsborough (Bayardo–Rosedrop, by St Frusquin).

On this evidence it was reasonable to hope that East Woodhay House, situated barely a quarter of a mile away and on similar land, might turn out to be equally suitable for breeding good racehorses. The fencing, paddocks and ditches needed a good deal of attention, but the land was not horse-sick, the stud yard was in good order and it possessed satisfactory housing for stud workers.

Studs in this category are fairly sound propositions, and economically are preferable to building new ones or converting existing properties or farms.

Provided money is no object and the land is suitable, forming a new stud on pastures which have never had horses on them is likely to be the best proposition of all, since horses thrive on fresh land and deteriorate markedly on land that is stale or horse-sick. The late Fred Myerscough, an outstanding judge of yearlings, once told a friend of mine that he only knew one cast-iron guide to buying yearlings and that was to find a draft bred on good land on which horses had never been reared before.

The breeder is therefore well advised to take the utmost trouble in finding out the nature and possibilities of the land, how it has been farmed and whether any good racehorses have been bred in the neighbourhood, before he contemplates any purchase. Besides having the land tested scientifically, it is wise to consult someone who has lived and farmed in the district for a considerable number of years and knows the peculiarities, attributes and shortcomings of the local soil. In making such inquiries it is advisable to pick on an individual who understands what is required in breeding racehorses, as opposed to fattening cattle or sheep. The eventual goal of the breeder of racehorses is the winner's enclosure, not the fatstock market.

In general, pastures should be well drained and the land neither too heavy nor too light. If it is too heavy the ground tends to become hock-deep in winter and hard as iron in summer, both extremes being equally undesirable as regards improving the action of foals and yearlings. If it is too light, horses reared on it are inclined to lack substance.

Sometimes the nature of the land varies from one part of the stud to another. This was the case on our stud, where several paddocks were on gravel, the rest being on a mixture of loam and clay. The former were ideal for winter grazing, as they never became heavy no matter how wet the weather, while the others provided good summer grazing.

Horses like shade from the sun and shelter from wind and rain. They appreciate paddocks with trees adjoining them, which give both shade and shelter, also hedges or belts of trees to break the force of the prevailing wind. A stud with nothing between its paddocks and the North Pole provides little comfort for its inhabitants. Horses do not thrive under such conditions and tend to be late coming to hand when sent into training. In such circumstances it is advisable to erect open sheds facing away from the prevailing wind, to supply shade and shelter in place of natural protection, though horses go into them more often in hot weather than when it is raining.

It is particularly important for a stud to be well drained if the land tends to hold the wet. This entails the paddocks being properly ditched and these being kept dug out and clear of weeds so that the water flows freely through them. Our own stud had ditches round the paddocks, which means a good deal of work keeping them in efficient order, since they must be dug out once a year.

An aspect of the utmost importance not always appreciated by breeders is that of a stud's water supply. For a study of this subject I would recommend an article entitled 'Water' by Dr John Burkhardt in the Summer 1971 issue of the *British Racehorse*.

The reason for the importance of water is that it is the chief source of calcium, without which good, sound bone cannot be grown in horses.

From a careful, practical research on studs which consistently produced stock with unsound legs – in particular, knees and fetlocks – and insufficient bone of poor quality, Dr Burkhardt discovered that the chief cause was lack of calcium or lime content in the drinking water.

Dr Burkhardt quotes the case of an eminent stud in France on which a well had to be dug to provide water, owing to the former supply having been destroyed by enemy action during the war. From then on, serious faults began to appear in the young stock: bowed forelegs, enlargements of the radius and knee bones and straightening of the fetlock joints were some of the troubles discerned.

Though hard, the water when tested revealed only a minimum of calcium, the hardness arising from the presence of magnesium.

To cope with the situation a plant was installed to feed calcium into the water supply and within a year the faults in the young stock were eliminated.

This emphasizes the great importance of water on a stud and, if enlargements and deformities start appearing in the young stock, of having the water tested at once in case lack of calcium proves to be the cause of the trouble.

The third way in which a breeder can operate his stud is that of boarding his mares, foals and yearlings on someone else's stud. (This is what we have done since selling East Woodhay House, our mares now being at the Warren Stud near Newmarket.)

This has its advantages and disadvantages, according to the situation of the breeder. If he can give his personal attention to his stud, or is operating on a big enough scale to employ a first-class manager, he will be better off with his own stud, since he has complete direction over the way in which it is run. If he boards his stock on another stud, he is not in any position to tell the owner how to run it any more than the parent of a child at boarding school is in a position to dictate to the headmaster regarding the running of the school. The higher the category of the stud, the stronger the position of its owner and the weaker that of the breeder patronizing it.

However, there are circumstances in which a breeder may not have the necessary knowledge, time and energy to run a stud himself; or he may have an insufficient number of mares to merit having a stud of his own; or he may live in an area which is not conducive to breeding racehorses; and so on.

If so placed he must look round for a stud where his stock will receive the best attention and which can produce good racehorses.

There are some studs which specialize in taking boarders and these can be satisfactory; but it is wise to investigate the stud thoroughly before patronizing it, to make sure that it is run on the scale of a first-class hotel and not a cheap boarding house. It is far better to pay a high price and have the stock really well looked after and fed, than to try to do it on the cheap. The golden rule about all aspects of racing and breeding is that whether you can afford it or not, money must be no obstacle when it comes to running a stud or having a horse in training. The situation to avoid is that of paying through the nose and not having the horses fed and looked after to a standard comparable to the price paid.

The ideal situation for a breeder wishing to board his mares out is to find a friend who owns a really good stud at which boarders are not taken in as a matter of course but who will make an exception as a favour. This is usually possible only if the breeder requiring a home for his stock has but a few mares. At our own stud we sometimes took a mare for Harry Oppenheimer, whose chief breeding interests are in South Africa, but we were not a boarding stud.

There is no reason, provided he chooses wisely, why a breeder boarding his stock out should not be successful. One such breeder who comes to mind is Walter Burmann, who lived in London and until giving up breeding in 1975 had his mares at the beautiful Haras du Quesnay in Normandy, owned by Alec Head. Notable winners under his colours bred at this stud include Bon Mot (Prix de l'Arc de Triomphe), Tidra (Prix de St Alary; 2nd French Oaks), Tennyson (Grand Prix de Paris) and Bonami, a good horse who unfortunately met with an accident which later proved fatal.

The 1975 Goodwood Stakes winner, Dubrovnik, was bred by his owner, Harry Oppenheimer, at our East Woodhay House Stud, as was his dam Hardiesse, who carried his colours to victory in the Cheshire Oaks, Prix Malleret and other races and finished fourth in the Oaks.

Thus the prospective owner-breeder has several avenues of possible success, but all must have the essential attributes of the right land and water, good feeding and proper management.

2

Planning for Racing

When the owner-breeder has produced his yearlings and sent them into training, his work is far from over, unless he has neither the knowledge nor the experience to do more than leave the whole matter to the trainer.

While it is one thing to leave the trainer alone to arrange all the practical side of a horse's training – if an owner has not sufficient confidence in the trainer to do this there is no point in sending him the horses – it is another to leave the planning of the horse's racing career entirely in his hands. To start with it is not much fun, and since, financially, a racehorse owner is usually on a good hiding to nothing, he might as well have some entertainment out of it. There is little amusement in having no idea when or where a horse is going to run until the day before the race, when an owner may have made an engagement from which he cannot extract himself, so is unable to get to the meeting. This suits many trainers. They don't have the owner round their necks all day at the races, possibly touting them as to the chances of their other horses, asking stupid questions, spoiling the market by telling all their friends and acquaintances that their horse is sure to win, blaming the trainer and/or the jockey if he does not and generally adding to the burden of life. On the whole, trainers favour clients who are millionaires living in another continent, pay their bills regularly, hardly ever come to England, do not bet, reward the yard generously in the case of victory and are quite content to read of an occasional success of one of their horses in the newspapers. However, such treasured patrons do not grow on trees and a trainer has to take the powder with the jam so far as run-of-the-mill patrons are concerned. These include the dedicated owner-breeder who takes a serious interest in the operation and, even if he does not expect to make money, is not particularly keen to go broke at it.

Nesbit Waddington, who for years managed the studs of the late Aga Khan and bred and raced horses with success on his own account, once remarked to me: 'If anyone wanting to breed and race horses asked my advice, the first thing I would tell him would be to find a good trainer.' There is wisdom in this advice, for no matter how good a horse may be, the most will not be made of him if he is badly trained and managed. Thus a good trainer is of paramount importance to an owner-breeder, as is the racing plan for his horses. Therefore it is extremely important for an owner-breeder not only to find a good trainer, but one with whom he can work, if he wishes to direct the race planning of his horse himself. There are plenty of trainers who are first class in the stable and on the gallops, but are weak when it comes to race planning, and vice versa. The owner-breeder who knows what he is about as regards choosing the right races for his horses and arranging their programme is therefore better off with a trainer of the former category than with one of the latter. Ideally the solution is a trainer who understands the principles behind an owner-breeder's policy and is skilled in the other aspects as well.

The policy of an owner-breeder is as different from that of an owner who does not breed as is that of a commercial breeder from one who breeds to race. Not all trainers appreciate this. While a non-breeding owner is out to win races and no more, apart from selling the horse later on and, if he is so inclined, betting on him, the owner-breeder wants to keep up the prestige of his stud and discover the true measure of his horses with regard to his future breeding plans. It is important to win a race with a horse, even if it is necessary to go to a small meeting to do so, but once this has been achieved there is no point in the owner-breeder trying to pick up another race of no consequence, for it will add little further prestige to the horse or his dam and her other stock, whereas defeat in such a race will knock some of the gilt off the gingerbread. Instead, it is wiser to fly higher, even if success is more unlikely. The reason for this is that a placing in a Group race or one of some value and importance will bring more prestige than victory in a sphere in which the horse has already proved himself. If he is beaten it will not entail loss of face, because he will have been racing in good company. Besides, it will show the breeder exactly how the horse stands in relation to good-class horses, which is a considerable help to future planning, both in mating and culling. When a horse has only raced in moderate company, even though he wins, it is not always easy to know his exact standing against good-class horses. This is especially important as regards fillies who may be returning to the stud. In former days this type of plan was unpopular with trainers, as they only received a percentage on winning horses and it offered no scope for betting, beyond the occasion of the horse being exploited in moderate class. Nowadays, apart from the betting aspect, trainers have little of which to complain from the point of view of running in good-class races, since they receive a percentage on place money, which in the case of valuable races amounts to more than winning small races. Thus our own filly Posy (Major Portion–Bell Crofts, by Arctic Time) earned nearly £1,000 for running second in the Nell Gwyn Stakes, about three times as much as she received for winning at Redcar the previous year.

The object of the owner-breeder is to enhance the merit of his stock, that of the owner who does not breed is to win what he can where he can, when he can and, if he bets seriously, to throw dust in the eyes of the handicapper, regardless of the effect on the horse's prestige, till the day comes for the horse to be unleashed.

Not only is race planning important to the owner-breeder, but also the entries in general. The very fact of putting a horse in a moderate race is an indication that little is thought of him, while it is sometimes possible to fluke a win in quite a good race, because it has dried up to a few runners, or at least gain a place in such an event.

In the case of an owner who likes to make his own entries, it is important to liaise closely with the trainer so that confusion is avoided. My experience is that the best method is to send the entry sheet, with one's entries written upon it, direct to the trainer, leaving him to make any additional entries he may think fit. By this method it is almost impossible to miss an opportunity. In the case of trainers who cannot be relied upon to make sensible entries, the latter stage is omitted. In general, trainers tend to fall into two categories: either they enter every horse in every race for which he is qualified, or they enter too unambitiously. With a top horse, it is better to be over-ambitious in the matter of entries than under-ambitious: you cannot put a horse in a race after it has closed and parsimony in entries can cost a fortune in missed opportunities.

The philosophy of a non-breeding owner is exactly the opposite. It is in his interests to make the handicapper think as little as possible of his horses.

Naturally there are occasions when it is in the interests of an owner-breeder to run in a small race or handicap, but victory in the latter will be of little benefit to the prestige of his stud unless it is a race of some value and standing. My experience is that if horses are raced completely openly, every now and then circumstances present a bonus in the shape of a horse thrown into a handicap. Some years ago we had a horse called Brigade Major (Major Portion–La Paiva, by Prince Chevalier) who showed useful form as a two-year-old without winning. At three he won a valuable maiden race at Kempton, following this up with a victory in the Cosmopolitan Cup, a handicap with a measure of prestige attached to it. He was sent to Nottingham in May for a smaller race, which he appeared likely to win. On arrival we found the going to be firmer than we wanted for him, but with a good covering of grass. We decided that he might as well take his chance, since he had sound legs and was unlikely to do himself any harm, his dislike of firm going being due to the fact that he had shelly feet. He ran appallingly, never striding out freely and clearly putting up a performance far below his true merit. We did not run the horse again until the Cambridgeshire; here the going was better than at Nottingham, but not soft enough to be ideal for him. He ran well until he was let down a couple of furlongs out, when he began to feel the ground and dropped out of contention, though he was by no means disgraced. The following year he was entered for the Great Jubilee Handicap at Kempton, in which he was given 8 st 5 lb, 18 lb less than his stable companion Colum. Shortly before the race Brigade Major worked with Colum giving him 3 lb and beating him half a length. Thus in the Jubilee, Brigade Major had 21 lb and half a length the best of the weights with Colum. At 16 to 1 in the ante-post betting he represented wonderful value for money and I had a good bet on him. Had it rained before the race I would have trebled my bet, but as the ground dried up somewhat, my courage failed me. He won convincingly and on soft ground would probably have done so by six lengths.

I am convinced that it is bad policy to prevent horses from doing their best, as it perplexes them mentally and may even lead them to believe that they are required to ease up some way before the end of the race. Many years ago there was a useful handicap hurdler, whose connections decided that they would put him by for a coup. He was stopped for a year, the process being to let him run along until the last hurdle but one and then drop him out. Eventually the day arrived and the money was put down. All went well until the last hurdle but one, when he dropped himself out, despite all the urging of his jockey. He continued to do this from then on, though eventually he did manage to win one bad seller in the west country, probably because he could not help it.

The planning of a horse's racing career begins long before he goes into training. The first stage is in the mating of his dam with his sire, for unless the breeder is operating completely haphazardly he has a particular objective in mind when he designs the mating. For instance, the specific object of snding La Paiva to Queen's Hussar was to produce an eight-to-ten-furlong horse, whose primary aim, should he prove good enough, was to be the Two Thousand Guineas; if a filly, the target would be the One Thousand Guineas. The result was Brigadier Gerard.

Since it is a considerable advantage to a Guineas horse to be well advanced, that he should be an early foal is preferable to his being a late one. In the case of a horse whose *métier* is to be among stayers, this is of little importance, since the older he becomes, the less is to be gained by being a month or two in advance of his rivals. In the bad old days it was an open secret that more than one Derby winner was a four-year-old. It was even rumoured that the triple crown winner Gladiateur was not his true age. Concerning this, Matthew Dawson is said to have answered to a query as to whether he thought the horse was a four-year-old, 'At least!' That Gladiateur was not a three-year-old is, however, doubtful.

Some breeders are prejudiced against January foals on the grounds that if the weather is bad their early days are liable to be spent in most uncongenial circumstances. Often they cannot go out in the paddock, there is no spring grass, little or no sun and the whole process is entirely against nature. The late Aga Khan liked his foals to be dropped if possible in April, which is the ideal month, being not too late to be a disadvantage in the matter of age, and not too early as regards the weather and spring grass.

Though not all the foaling dates of Derby winners are available, in comparatively recent times the following January foals have gone on to win the Derby: Gainsborough, Captain Cuttle, Manna, Cameronian, St Paddy and Larkspur. Since January foals are in the minority, this is quite a significant tally. While it is not worth risking a mating which might involved the foal being born the previous December, a service date which involves the mare foaling in January, February or March is certainly worth considering if the chief aim is to breed a Guineas, Derby or Oaks winner. Brigadier Gerard, who was well advanced in development as both a two- and a three-year-old, was foaled on 4 March.

One of the most difficult tasks of the owner-breeder is to assess his horses objectively. There is a strong temptation to view one's geese as swans and to relate a horse's prospects to the quality of his pedigree rather than to the merit he shows on his home gallops and – what is more important – on the racecourse.

The way in which yearlings gallop in the paddock can be deceptive, since some are lazy while others are free; but when two individuals appear to be similar in character, precocity and type, paddock performance is sometimes reproduced accurately on the racecourse later. This certainly proved so with Fille de Joie (Midsummer Night II–La Paiva, by Prince Chevalier) and Eleanor Bold (Queen's Hussar–Bell Crofts, by Arctic Time), since the former always was too fast for the latter when they were yearlings and proved a class superior to her on the racecourse. Both were free-going, active fillies, eager to race, and enjoyed vying with each other in the paddock.

On the other hand, it is dangerous to condemn a horse until he has been thoroughly tested on the racecourse, however slow he appears at home, or however badly he moves. Some horses simply will not extend themselves until aroused by the excitement of the racecourse – Hyperion was one – and as a result probably need a race or two to get them fully fit. Thus, however unpromising a horse may appear as a yearling or before he races, he should be entered for the events for which he has been bred. If he is not considered worth this, it is better not to send him into training at all. To send a classically bred horse into training and not enter him accordingly is to chance missing a golden opportunity. This proved the case with Vaguely Noble (Vienna–Noble Lassie, by Nearco), who turned out to be the best mile-and-a-half horse in Europe, but was given no classic engagements. It is always possible to strike a horse out of the Derby if he has been entered, but not to put him in after the entries have closed, unless he can be supplemented, which is costly.

Horses bred to win as two-year-olds and those of top-class ability, even if they have staying pedigrees, almost invariably show speed as soon as they are put into fast work in the spring. A 'Yorkshire gallop' in March or early April will usually sort out the sheep from the goats and enable a provisional plan to be made for each individual. If a two-year-old has a precocious pedigree and shows no particular ability, but it is evident that he has come to hand, it is as well to get on with him and win as much as possible before the better ones come out. He can then be rested and brought out later in the season when the nurseries begin, or be sold on his performance.

If a two-year-old is sprinting bred and promises to be in or near the top class his progress can be more gradual since, rightly, the value of two-year-old races increases as the season progresses; and there is no point, other than for betting, in using up horses by winning insignificant races early in the season. Many a valuable race has been thrown away by exploiting a horse too early in the season, so that by the time the more important events come round he has been used up.

Much depends upon the individual. A really tough horse, physically and mentally, can sometimes survive a formidable programme, starting in the first week of racing; but as a general principle the best is made of a horse if he begins his racing career gradually, with not too many or severe races as a two-year-old, his races becoming more frequent and testing as he grows older. In this respect the programme of Brigadier Gerard may be of interest:

Two Years

24 June	Berkshire Stakes, Newbury, £1,201. 5 furlongs. Won
2 July	Champagne Stakes, Salisbury, £598. 6 furlongs. Won
15 August	Washington Singer Stakes, Newbury, £1,154. 6 furlongs. Won
1 October	Middle Park Stakes, Newmarket, £10,515. 6 furlongs. Won

Three Years

1 May	The Two Thousand Guineas, Newmarket, £27,283. 1 mile. Won
15 June	St James's Palace Stakes, Royal Ascot, £4,857. 1 mile. Won
28 July	Sussex Stakes, Goodwood, £12,134. 1 mile. Won
28 August	Goodwood Mile, Goodwood, £3,926. 1 mile. Won
25 September	Queen Elizabeth II Stakes, Ascot, £5,761. 1 mile. Won
16 October	Champion Stakes, Newmarket, £25,279. 1 mile 2 furlongs. Won

Four Years

20 May	Lockinge Stakes, Newbury, £7,249. 1 mile. Won
29 May	Westbury Stakes, Sandown, £2,253. 1 mile 2 furlongs. Won
20 June	Prince of Wales Stakes, Royal Ascot, £8,221. 1 mile 2 furlongs. Won
8 July	Eclipse Stakes, Sandown, £32,579. 1 mile 2 furlongs. Won
21 July	King George VI and the Queen Elizabeth II Stakes, Ascot, £60,202. 1 mile 4 furlongs. Won
15 August	Benson & Hedges Gold Cup, York, £30,955. 1 mile 2 furlongs and 110 yards. Second
23 September	Queen Elizabeth II Stakes, Ascot, £5,658. 1 mile. Won
14 October	Champion Stakes, Newmarket, £35,048. 1 mile 2 furlongs. Won

From his first gallop as a two-year-old, on 4 April, it was clearly evident that the Brigadier had considerable merit and could have run any time from then onwards. Had he been exploited as a two-year-old, it is doubtful whether he would have progressed as he did, since, though he had come to hand early and was fast, he was still immature. As a two-year-old he was 16 hands, at three 16.1 hands and at four 16.2 hands. Thus a severe programme in his first season might have prejudiced his future.

At all costs the temptation to over-race a two-year-old who is likely to benefit from a gradual programme is to be avoided, even if he has shown early brilliance.

On the other hand, if a horse is not bred to stay more than six or seven furlongs and shows early brilliance it is as well to make the most of him as a two-year-old, as he will not find comparable opportunities later in life. A typical example is My Swallow, a precocious horse and a brilliant two-year-old, who never reproduced his true form after the Two Thousand Guineas, in which his running with Mill Reef was in accordance with their form in the previous season's Prix Robert Papin, bearing in mind the advantage of the draw enjoyed by My Swallow that day.

Bad and moderate horses have got to win where they can, when they can and if they can. Once their best distance and the going they favour has been discovered, the wisest plan is to have them well entered and to pull them out when a suitable opportunity presents itself.

The higher the class of horse, the more important does planning become. That is to say, if the most is to be made of him, as opposed to racing him for purely social reasons and amusement. 'I want to have a runner in the Derby' has been the death knell to the racing career of many a useful horse below classic standard.

One of the basic principles of planning a high-class horse's career is to let the horse tell you he is ready to run, rather than run him merely for the sake of getting him out. Unless a horse is obstreperous, or there is some other good reason for doing so, there is little or nothing to be gained by bringing out a promising two-year-old before he is advanced enough to have a chance of finishing in the first three. If sent out merely to go down and come back, he may get the idea that this is all he is required to do; or if he is a free-going horse, he may over-exert himself when not in a condition to have a hard race.

At the highest level, bringing a horse out too early may result in besmirching his record with a defeat that was not necessary. I can think of at least two classic winners whom this fate befell.

It should be borne in mind that a two-year-old who is some way below peak fitness will be meeting rivals who have been tuned right up, been tried at home and have fought out a finish on the racecourse. He will be at a great disadvantage with such as these, and the earlier the date at which he meets them, the greater will be the disadvantage under which he labours. If, on the other hand, his debut is delayed until mid-summer or later, the work he has done at home will have been over a longer period and will have increased steadily in tempo, so that by the time he comes out he will be fit to do himself justice and still have scope for improvement. Should it be thought desirable to widen his experience before he appears in public, it is sometimes possible to give him a gallop on a racecourse after racing, but a trainer who knows his business should be able to produce a two-year-old sufficiently educated to render a reasonably good account of himself first time out on home work alone.

The earlier in the year that a horse starts training and racing, the more it takes out of him, because he will be stripped and exerted in cold weather. This may mean that he will not retain his form throughout the season and raises a problem as regards the programme of a candidate for either of the Guineas races. A sluggish horse who is not a free worker at home will almost certainly need a preliminary race before the Guineas. This applies more to colts than fillies, the former usually being tougher than the latter, who tend to be more adversely affected by a cold spring.

On the other hand, if a colt is a free worker at home, the longer he is kept off the racecourse during the early part of the year, the more likely he is to retain his form throughout the season. Besides, a hard race before the Two Thousand Guineas will prejudice a horse's chance on the day, especially in the case of a free mover who is not particularly robust, or in heavy going. In France the situation is rather different, since the so-called trial races for the classics are extremely valuable and carry considerable prestige, victory in one of them being an acceptable consolation for subsequent failure in a classic.

The keenness of many trainers to give a Two Thousand Guineas horse a race before the day is sometimes due as much to inability to assess the candidate's state of fitness accurately without seeing him perform in public as to the need of a horse for such an outing.

Discussing the plan for Brigadier Gerard with Dick Hern and Joe Mercer before the Two Thousand, we came to the conclusion that nothing was to be gained by running him beforehand. It would have meant either taking on one of his chief opponents, Mill Reef and My Swallow, for peanuts, or running him earlier than was desirable in view of the fact that his eventual target for that season was the Champion Stakes. However easily he wins, a horse has something taken out of him in a top-class race. According to the severity of the struggle, the time between this race and his next engagement must be carefully gauged. A horse may eat up, look well, work well at home, weigh the amount he should and still not have recovered completely. This can only be discovered on the racecourse and affects a three-year-old more than one four years or older. Though Brigadier Gerard was a horse of steel and did not have a hard race in the King George VI and Queen Elizabeth Stakes and was a four-year-old, the Ascot race took something out of him which was not discernible, so that when asked to quicken for a finishing run in the Benson and Hedges Gold Cup he could not do so and suffered the only defeat of his career. A further factor operating against him, and only evident after the race, was that, on returning to the stables and putting his head down, a large clot of mucus came out of one of his nostrils, so his breathing in the race had been impaired.

The horses behind him were beaten out of sight and it was excusable to be unable to foresee that the winner was going to produce over a stone of improvement on his last running, out of the hat. Even so, the principle of the policy was wrong and my decision to run him, made against the inclination of my partner and the advice of an old friend of great experience, was an error of judgement.

The lesson was driven home once again when Grundy failed to reach the first three in the Benson and Hedges Gold Cup of 1975. In his case the danger signs were more evident, as he was only a three-year-old and had had a crucifying race in the King George VI and Queen Elizabeth Stakes, being stone cold when he pulled up.

The late Matt Peacock used to say that after a hard race in top-class company a horse needed six weeks before he raced again; and the late Dick Dawson once told me that for a month after he had won the Derby, Trigo would not have won a seller. He did not produce the horse on a racecourse again until the St Leger, which Trigo won.

There is a strong tendency among owners and trainers to run top-class horses, especially three-year-olds, too often. This is due to the lure of the prize money and, sometimes, to the decision to retire the horse at the end of his three-year-old career and the resultant desire to get as much as possible out of him in the season. As often as not, a penalty has to be paid for going to the well once too often. Another victim of such a fate was Nijinsky, who, after winning the St Leger following recovery from a skin ailment, had a desperately hard race in the Prix de l'Arc de Triomphe, in which he was just beaten by Sassafras, and then contested the Champion Stakes, where he was again beaten, being a nervous wreck by the time he got to the post.

Before the race Evan Williams, who won the Grand National on Royal Mail and trained Supreme Court, winner of the first King George VI and Queen Elizabeth Stakes, was looking at Nijinsky in the paddock. A connection of the stable remarked that since his return from France the horse had eaten up, worked well and was back to his best racing weight. Evan, a good judge of a horse – and a hound – replied to the effect that he may have put the weight back, but in the wrong place, not over his back and loins. This underlines the importance of judgement by eye, rather than reliance on weight. A trainer who knows his job does not need a weighing machine to tell him how his horse is and whether he is at his correct weight or not. While a weighing machine is useful up to a point, it is dangerous to place too much reliance on it.

An important aspect of planning a horse's racing programme is travelling. If a horse is a bad traveller, a long journey takes far more out of him than a race. The reason why horses in America can run so often is that they have no travelling to do when they are at a meeting, which goes on for several weeks; they only have to walk from their stable a few yards onto the racecourse. Unfortunately a horse's reaction to travel can only be discovered by trial and error; some actually enjoy travelling, but these are in the minority. Thus it is advisable to start off a horse's racing career fairly near home, extending his journeys according to his reaction to travelling. In general, two-year-olds need their con-fidence building up as regards travelling and unless showing remarkable disregard to being carted about the country, it is preferable not to send them to race abroad until they are three or, at least, until the last race of their juvenile season. One of the snags of overseas travel is all the delays and red tape at airports. If a nervous two-year-old has an unhappy experience travelling, it may shake his confidence and, consequently, affect his racing performance.

The reason why we ran Brigadier Gerard in the Champagne Stakes at Salisbury as opposed to the July Stakes at Newmarket – this being only his second race – was that it was closer to home and did not entail a night away. In fact he proved a good traveller, but the precautions taken in his early races may have contributed towards this.

Another aspect of the effect of travelling on a horse's racing performance is that of staying overnight in a strange box. This has a disastrous effect on some horses, as they fret and do not relax, even though they may eat up; consequently they run far below form. With horses such as these, the only solution is to send them early on the day of the race. One such horse was the 1975 Mackeson Gold Cup chase winner Clear Cut, who left his stable in Yorkshire at 5 a.m. on the morning of the race. Another is the 1991 Derby winner, Generous, who flew to Ireland on the morning of the Irish Derby, which he won.

Since peculiarities of this kind can only be discovered by experiment, it is as well to send a horse for a race overnight, after he has had a couple of runs as a two-year-old, to see how he reacts; the resulting information might make the difference between winning and losing a classic later on.

The more knowledge a breeder has about the peculiarities of a horse from which he intends to breed, the better chance he has of mating him or her with success. Thus he should keep in close touch with his trainer on the matter of his horse's behaviour in and out of the stable, to find out whether he is a good doer or is delicate, is nervous or fretful, bad tempered or mulish, has any physical or constitutional weakness, etc.

While an owner should not interfere with a trainer as regards the way he runs his stable and feeds and works his horses, it is a mistake to let a trainer interfere with the stud. Few trainers understand breeding and all tend to be prejudiced either against or in favour of members of certain families, male or female, often basing their view on their experience with only one horse. 'I never want to see another Tudor Melody in my yard,' one trainer somewhat surprisingly observed of this extremely successful sire because the only horse by him he had ever trained happened to be a bad one.

No more successful Turf relationship existed than that between the late Lord Rosebery and his trainer the late Sir Jack Jarvis, yet Lord Rosebery never discussed his stud with his trainer.

The larger the enterprise, be it a racing stable or a stud, the more difficult it becomes to study each horse individually. As a result, in a large concern some horses do not do as well as they should, opportunities are missed and standards tend to be lowered. I have noticed, with rare exceptions, that the standards of turn-out and general appearance of horses in racing stables and studs are apt to be inversely proportional to the number of horses in the stable or stud. This does not matter much to the trainer; he can give his personal attention to the best horses, which are the real wage-earners, while the others take their chance under the eye of his assistant – if he has one – help to defer the costs of running the stable and are handy as cannon-fodder in the shape of leading work. In an efficiently run, well-staffed, big stable this works well enough, but if the machinery is not well oiled, things can get in a pretty good muddle. Whether a trainer has twenty horses or a hundred, there are still only the same number of hours into which to fit the morning's work and evening inspection. In the hustle and bustle of getting through a work morning, I have known a batch of horses come up the gallop unobserved because the trainer has forgotten all about them. It is impossible to go round a hundred horses properly at evening stables. Besides, out at exercise there is little time to watch carefully how each horse trots out when he pulls up or blows as he walks back to be rugged up. The trainer either has to take the word of one of his staff or, if he wants to pay particular attention to the horses in a gallop, must forgo seeing the next batch come up.

In the end it probably all comes out in the wash. You cannot make bad horses into good ones; if a horse goes well, his rider will not be slow to say so; if he goes badly, the truth will out sooner or later; and if he breaks down it will be self-evident. Racehorses are remarkably tolerant and adaptable, and if well fed and given reasonable exercise once a day and some sort of stronger work twice a week, will probably win in their turn, which is all that the average owner hopes for.

The dedicated owner-breeder does not find this quite so satisfactory. While it is necessary to view with a measure of tolerance the difficulties, physical and financial, of modern training, an owner in this category likes to see his horse given the best chance possible. Therefore it is no bad plan, if he is in a large and fashionable stable, to send his moderate horses to a smaller yard, always provided it is well run. Otherwise he may find his moderate horses in a big stable being ignored, or ground to powder leading someone else's Group I candidates.

Highly strung or nervous horses usually do better in small yards, where the tempo is less hectic and more time can be spent on them.

I heard of one owner removing his horse from a large stable because the trainer did not know it by sight. Be that as it may, it is up to an owner to find a trainer who suits him and, if it does not work out, try another.

In these days of viruses running through stables like wildfire and perhaps putting the string virtually out of action for the season, it is not a bad idea for an owner to spread his horses among two or more stables, according to the size of his string.

On the Turf nowadays sport tends to be spelt with a small 's' and commercialism with a large 'C'. Thus the inclination is for good three-year-olds to be whisked out of training and syndicated before they can be 'found out' by competition with the younger generation as four-year-olds. This is against the best interests of racing and breeding. It takes much enjoyment out of racing and deprives the breeder of information which is of great value when it comes to assessing a horse as a stallion. In the case of a three-year-old taken out of training, it is not possible to tell whether he has trained on, either as regards his temperament or his performance, or how he compares with the younger generation, or whether he has improved relatively from three to four, or whether his legs are able to stand up to an extra season's racing and whether, if he has ended his three-year-old career with a defeat, his morale has been affected. Not unnaturally, more reputations are dented than enhanced by keeping classic winners in training as four-year-olds and the horse thus misses a season at stud, so it is not surprising that a good many are retired at the end of their three-year-old season. Notable horses in this category since the war, excluding such as Pinza and Crepello who broke down, embrace Tulyar, Santa Claus, Sea Bird II, Sir Ivor, Nijinsky, Vaguely Noble, Grundy and Nashwan.

The only means of arresting this trend would be for breeders to refuse to pay high prices for shares in, or nominations to, such horses, but since not a few of the purchasers acquire them as much to trade in the nominations and shares as to use them to try to breed good horses, there is little danger of so altruistic a situation developing.

Planning a horse's career to include a season as a four-year-old is of especial benefit to a big or late-developing horse and a stayer. Such horses are likely to prove relatively better at four than at three. Racing a horse on as a four-year-old is usually of greater advantage to horses bred in Europe than in the USA where horses tend to come to hand earlier, perhaps on account of their getting more sunshine and being selectively bred to do so, and to be more developed at an early age than European-bred horses; but on the whole the American horses do not seem to improve so much from three to four as do their European counterparts. Though Mill Reef's form as a four-year-old cannot be taken at face value, because he was not himself that year, he did not grow a fraction from the previous year, whereas Brigadier Gerard grew an inch.

We live in an age of specialization, which in racing means that there is a tendency to keep horses within a narrow margin of distance in their races. Thus the established miler will seldom race beyond this distance or short of seven furlongs, the middle-distance horse is kept to races of ten to twelve furlongs and the stayer to one and three-quarter miles or further. But a really good horse excels at all distances and, if trained with versatility in mind, is capable of winning at all distances. In the past, when there was no financial lure to go to France and a horse's scope within a specialized distance was therefore limited, programmes for top horses were much more varied in the matter of the distances over which they raced. Thus the St Leger winner Fairway won from seven furlongs to over two miles as a four-year-old, and Royal Minstrel, an Eclipse Stakes (one and a quarter miles) winner, was narrowly beaten in the Nunthorpe Stakes (five furlongs) and the July Cup (six furlongs).

There is no reason why a top-class horse should not race over a variety of distances today if his owner feels so inclined, provided his speed is not blunted by working him regularly over long distances at home. Though Brigadier Gerard won the King George VI and the Queen Elizabeth Stakes over one and a half miles, he never worked beyond a mile at home, so that the edge was not taken off his speed and he was able to revert to a mile and break the record for this distance on the Ascot Old Mile course. Had he not had an unusually hard race in heavy going in the St James's Palace Stakes, the intention was to run him in the July Cup (six furlongs) at Newmarket.

The advantage of running a top horse on as a four-year-old is that his career can be planned so that his races at three can be spread out evenly, thus making it easier to bring him to the post at his best for each one. If it is thought desirable to run him in several races in quick succession, he should have a longer rest after the last of the series than if his races had had more time between them, especially if he is a three-year-old; otherwise there is a risk of his going over the top and incurring an unnecessary defeat.

The high feeding necessary to a racehorse is a considerable strain on his liver and digestion. He will therefore benefit from being let down for a spell some time during the season, with his corn reduced, to give his liver and digestion a chance to rest. An interval of four weeks between top races makes it possible for him to be given a short respite, but if he is going to be pulled out two or three times with only a week intervening this is not practicable.

The prosperity of French racing, which since the war has gradually increased, has widened the scope for race planning, at the same time as complicating it. The lure of French prize money is attractive, but falling for it is not always in the best interests of a top horse. For him prestige is worth more than cash and there is no point in going to France purely for a bit more money, unless it is to take on a specific horse, the defeat of which would bring appreciable merit. For instance, there would have been little point in sending Brigadier Gerard to contest the Prix Jacques le Marois or the Prix du Moulin, since he had already beaten the best French milers in England.

In the present economic climate of England, more and more English owners are drifting to France, as French owners drifted to England between the two wars. This is understandable, but not necessarily the best solution for an owner-breeder unless he wishes to live in France. It is preferable for an owner to have his top horses under his eye in England, sending them over for selected French races if and when he wishes to do so; but it may well be worth while sending to France one or more horses of lesser class, who would be unlikely to pay their way in England but would almost certainly do so in France. Some owners find that by this system they are able to pay for their racing in England, but for which they would not be able to race at all.

English racing has certainly suffered by owners moving their entire strings to France, but by keeping the best in England and some of the others in France, an owner achieves a happy medium, which may well suit him socially as well as economically.

An owner on a big scale or fortunate enough to have two top horses of the same age and category will virtually be forced to include France in his planning, otherwise his horses will be opposing each other in the same race.

Conflict of interests in a stable is a delicate matter. Trainers tend to try to avoid top horses belonging to different owners clashing in the same race; this pleases the owners of horses inferior to the star of the stable and brings in more in percentages but is not not always in the interest of the owner of the star horse which, if allowed to contest them, would probably win all the best races at the expense of his lesser stable companions. By my book, if an owner is lucky enough to have an outstanding horse he is entitled to make the most of him; he will be unlikely ever to have another and his stable companions can either take him on or go for another race. With lesser horses and races it is a different matter. There is no point in two owners knocking their heads together for peanuts at Wolverhampton when one of them could go to Warwick instead. In fact, when Brigadier Gerard was a four-year-old we had intended to let his stable companion Sun Prince (Princely Gift–Costa Sola, by Worden II) run for the Queen Elizabeth II Stakes instead of him and it was only as a result of Sun Prince meeting with a mishap that the Brigadier took his place.

In big stables it is difficult to avoid clashes even in small races, which sometimes cause red faces and mixed feelings: it is not particularly entertaining for an owner who has had a decent bet on his horse in a maiden plate to see him beaten by a stable companion starting at 33 to 1.

Nowadays the staff in any good racing stable are well looked after, but it makes a big difference to a lad if the owner takes some interest in him, knows his name, tells him when his horse is likely to run and what the plan for him is. In the past, when

betting was a prominent factor, secrecy took a high priority in
most stables. In one stable none of the staff knew the names of
the horses until they had run: they were referred to by the
numbers of their boxes. One shrewd trainer informed his owner:
'Don't take any notice of what I say about your horses in the
letters typed by my secretary. You only want to pay attention
to the letters I write myself.' The training gallops were scanned
with field-glasses for touts before important gallops, stable lads
caught tipping were sacked on the spot, work riders were
equipped with lead-weighted waistcoats to deceive others in a
trial, and so on. When Spearmint was tried for the Derby, which
he won, the touts waited from dawn for days at the back gate at
Clarehaven in order not to miss the gallop; but the first they
knew of it was when they encountered the horses returning
after the trial. They had been taken out through the paddock
behind the yard, across Lord Derby's private ground, a section
of the railings having been removed to let them through, and
galloped on Waterhall while the touts were still at the back
gate.

With betting on a big scale a thing of the past, subterfuges of
this kind are a waste of time nowadays. In any case, the more
open an owner is about his horses, the less notice is taken of
what he says and the better the price. There is far more to be
gained by keeping a lad interested in his horse than in telling
him nothing.

There is one point concerning top-class racing at international
level that is important. Provided a horse is being given a good
interval between races, it is not a bad plan for him to be hand-
ridden right out each time he runs. Unless a horse is really
stretched, he will not reach that peak of fitness necessary to
success in international competition. This can only be done
satisfactorily on the racecourse, since attempting to do so at
home tends to sour a good horse by asking of him severe tasks
and to finish off relays of lead horses.

3

Engaging Staff

Having acquired his stud, the breeder must now set about putting it in action.

I once asked a successful practical breeder what he considered the order of priorities in running a stud. He replied: (1) personnel – their skill and sympathy with horses; (2) correct water and land; (3) feeding; (4) general management; (5) selection in the purchase of breeding stock; and (6) designing matings.

The key man on the stud, apart from the owner and/or manager, is the stud groom. He corresponds to the head lad in a racing stable or the sergeant-major in a military unit. He is responsible under the owner or manager for the day-to-day working of the stud, direction of the stud workers, feeding, care of the stock and farming of the paddocks. On a stud at which there is a stallion, the stud groom's task is more onerous, because he is responsible for the working management of the stallion, for the visiting mares, liaison with the veterinary surgeon, coping with mare owners and visitors and so on.

I have no experience of the stallion side of the business, so will confine myself to the aspect of a private stud where there is no stallion and the mares are foaled away, which is the only facet of which I have practical knowledge. There are excellent books on the management of stallions and the foaling of mares, reference to some of which will be found in the appendix.

The type of stud groom required depends upon the category of the stud. It is no use engaging a high-powered stud groom whose aim is a position on a top-class stud at which one or more stallions stand if the breeder has only a small, private stud without a stallion, however willing and able a worker the applicant may be. Understandably, when he sees the chance of a job in line with his ambition he will take it and the breeder will have to begin a search for a stud groom all over again.

Soon after we started the East Woodhay House Stud and were looking for a stud groom, an applicant came to see me about the job; and although he had had no previous experience on a

Thoroughbred stud he clearly possessed exceptional qualities and promise. Much as I would like to have employed him, I realized that there was not sufficient scope for him on a small, private stud with no stallion and that he would sooner or later want to improve his lot and thus would be far better placed on a top-class stud where there was an opportunity for advancement. I explained this to him and was able to find him a position on one of the best studs in England, where he became stud groom.

Not everyone wants the worry and responsibility of a high-powered stud, which either stands a top-class stallion or prepares expensive yearlings for sale, or both. Those in this category, provided they are good workers and otherwise suitable, fit into a private stud much better than a man with high ambitions. In reverse, if tempted, perhaps by good wages and other inducements, to take the post of stud groom on a big stud, a man of a less ambitious nature more often than not finds the strain of coping with the responsibilities too much for him and falls down on the job or decides to leave and find a less onerous position.

Thus the breeder should weigh up carefully the exact nature of the job which his future stud groom is to fill, decide on the type of man best suited to it and when he interviews him explain in detail every aspect of the position. It is no good engaging a stud groom, having given the impression that the job entails only looking after mares, foals, the paddocks and stud yard, and then expecting him to groom and exercise a couple of hunters, and clean out the chicken house as well.

While a good stud groom on a big stud will be prepared to take his coat off and help out with the less glamorous tasks if need be, the nature of his job is such that he will not often have time to do so, and certainly not in the covering season. On the other hand, on a small stud it is no use having a stud groom who is not prepared to do ordinary stud work, because he will not have enough to do otherwise.

Thus on a small stud it is advisable to advertise for a 'working stud groom' as opposed to just a 'stud groom'. He or she will still be in charge, but will work alongside the other staff.

A breeder with no knowledge of the business, or who cannot spend much time on the stud, is well advised to employ a stud manager who really knows the job. This is both in his own interest and in that of his stud groom and staff, as in the absence of the owner some crisis may arise placing an unfair responsibility on the stud groom and staff; while, human nature being what it is, irregularities are less likely to occur when supervision is present. As the late Tom Masson once observed to me, 'Everyone is straight with careful looking after.'

In the case of a small stud, a part-time manager will suffice and, in fact, the use of one in this category is a common practice.

If a manager is employed, his position must be made absolutely clear to the stud groom, to the staff and to the manager. In the absence of the owner, the manager is the former's representative and should carry full authority in all but major decisions. If he gives an instruction, it should be regarded by the stud groom and the staff as if it had been issued by the owner himself. In the case of a dispute, the owner should support his manager, unless he disapproves strongly of the action, in which circumstance it will probably be best to dispense with the manager's services altogether. If the owner does not support his manager, the latter's authority will be undermined and the whole object of employing him will be lost.

Apart from the aspect of supervising the men on the stud, the manager should direct the farming of the paddocks, repairs, buy the corn and hay and generally keep an eye on the business side and practical running of the stud.

If the owner is completely ignorant of the subject, the manager will have to help with, or be responsible for, the choice of nominations and shares in stallions, the purchase and disposal of breeding stock and the mating of the mares. When the owner knows little of the subject or is away for long periods at a time, the responsibilities of a stud manager are very considerable and the success or failure of the stud is largely in his hands. Therefore he must be an expert at the job, of high integrity and have the knack of getting on with men working under him.

The smaller the enterprise – whether it be a stud farm or any other business – the easier it is to assemble a good team of workers. This is essential to success and an agreeable atmosphere, and a man who disrupts this is better replaced, however tedious the process, than kept on.

Today labour relations can be frustrating and detrimental to progress. High wages are not necessarily the dominant factor in a stud worker's life, though it is unreasonable to expect anyone to work for inadequate payment. They like to know how they stand, be able to take a personal interest in the business, apart from profiting directly from its success, and have confidence that the owner or manager knows what he is about, thus feeling that the most is being made of the stock bred on the place.

Employers in general could profit by taking a leaf out of Field Marshal Montgomery's notebook, in that he firmly believed in putting his men fully in the picture before a battle. On a stud, this entails letting them know the stallions to whom the mares are going, what plans have been made for the foals and yearlings, the trainers to which they are going, the races at which they are likely to be aimed, and the running plans and chances of the horses when the time comes for them to race.

The larger the concern, the more difficult is this to achieve, which is one advantage of a small, private stud under the direct management of the owner.

On a large stud, jobs tend to become specialized: the stud groom and second man have their specific tasks, as do the stallion men, those who do the tractor work and those who deal chiefly with the yearlings and so on.

On a small stud the work is much more dovetailed and it is a great help if tasks are interchangeable. For instance, on our own stud, which employed three permanent men, with the addition of casual labour, all three drove a tractor. Thus tractor work was not held up as would be the case if only one could drive the tractor and he was on holiday.

Having secured a stud groom, the stud owner's next task is to engage the necessary number of stud workers.

In the matter of engaging stud workers, the stud groom should be consulted, since he will have them working with him and under his supervision. When advertising for a stud groom or stud worker I have found that *Horse and Hound* is the best medium, with, perhaps, in the case of a stud worker the addition of an advertisement in the local paper. The advertisement should run for three or four weeks, or at least for a couple of weeks and, if there is no reply after a week's interval, it should be repeated for another couple of weeks. Possible applicants might miss the first two advertisements, but see one of the subsequent ones.

A stud worker need not necessarily be experienced in this branch of occupation; if the individual is keen, industrious and has a way with animals, he soon picks up the job. Some of the best stud workers have come from varied backgrounds, such as racing stables or farms.

The same goes for student workers on a casual basis; these can be useful in such tasks as mowing, tractor work and fencing, leaving the work with horses to the regular staff.

The number of men employed on a stud depends upon the standard the owner wishes to maintain and the amount of money he is prepared to expend, but it is not possible to maintain a high standard with an insufficient staff.

Work to be done on a stud never ceases if the owner sets a high standard; and it is better, if finances allow, to be over-staffed than under-staffed, so that a backlog of work does not build up when men are away sick or on holiday.

If the stud owner is prepared to work himself when the opportunity occurs, it makes it easier for the team to keep the place in good order, as there is always scope for such jobs as mowing, edging the grass verges and cutting down thistles or nettles, which have a habit of springing up when one's back is turned and spoil the look of the place.

An insufficient staff cannot be expected to keep the place spick and span, as well as do the essential work; and while the care of the horses and paddocks must come first, nothing is more depressing than the sight of weeds, thistles, nettles and unkempt drives or paths, even if these do not affect the stock directly. Studmen appreciate a well-kept place, as they can display it with personal pride to their friends and relatives or to visitors.

Some men are naturally more tidy-minded than others and it may take a certain amount of persuasion to get anyone to change his nature. I once was much troubled by a stud worker who would not keep his own garden tidy, this being one of the terms of his employment. The situation was much improved by my doing his garden myself and knocking the overtime rates for my labour off his wages.

Nowadays a stud owner will only get the best results if he takes a close personal interest in his stud and spends most of his time there, or has a good manager who will fill his place when he is away. It is very depressing for men who work for an absentee stud owner or one who takes little interest in the place beyond the accounts, does not know one mare from another or the names of the men working for him.

Stud owners operating on a big scale naturally cannot have the same personal touch as those with a small stud, so that it is essential for them to have a good manager who can keep his employer fully informed about everything, as a good chief of staff does his commanding officer. Then, when the owner goes round his stud he has the necessary information at his finger-tips to be able to take an intelligent interest in his bloodstock and employees.

In all work concerning horses it is essential that those dealing with them should be patient, sympathetic and good tempered towards them. Any member of staff who proves to be rough, neglectful or unkind towards the horses should be dismissed immediately.

4

Selection of Breeding Stock

Having acquired his stud and engaged his staff, the breeder now arrives at the stage of assembling his breeding stock.

He has several avenues open to him. The purchase of a mare already at stud; that of a filly in or out of training; a yearling filly; a filly foal; or a collection from all these categories.

Sometimes the opportunity arises to acquire the whole breeding stock from a stud whose owner has died or given up breeding. Such an opportunity, if the stud and stock in question are of good quality, is the best proposition of all. In the case of a private executor's sale, the transaction usually takes place at probate value, which is invariably below market value, and the buyer can go through the stock carefully, decide what he wants to keep and sell the surplus. It is not unknown for the sale of the surplus to pay for the whole of the original purchase. I cannot think of any notable purchase of this nature that has not turned out well for the buyer.

Some instances of successful takeover purchases to come to mind are those by Marcel Boussac of the studs of Edmond Blanc and, later, of Evrémond de St Alary, that of the late Sir Victor Sassoon's studs by Louis Freedman and the acquisition by Sir Michael Sobell of the late Dorothy Paget's Ballymacoll Stud and bloodstock. Opportunities of this kind do not occur often and not every breeder can afford to buy on a scale necessary to make use of them, but to acquire a ready-made stud and its mares, foals, yearlings and possibly stallions as well is the best short-cut to starting as a breeder, provided the stud and stock are of sufficiently high quality and are managed properly by the buyer.

In the present financial climate of Great Britain, ready-made studs are likely to come onto the market more frequently, but whether breeders among English taxpayers will be found to buy and keep them up is another matter. At any rate, there are dispersal sales taking place from time to time, at which a breeder on a fairly modest scale can often pick up a mare or filly with a reasonable prospect of her making a foundation mare.

As in all aspects of breeding, there are no set rules or guides to finding good stock. Bad racemares, ill-shaped ones, unsound mares, mares with obscure pedigrees, bad-tempered mares, delicate mares – all from these unpromising categories have at some time or other produced a good racehorse. An occurrence of this kind is journalistic news and as such receives undue prominence in the press. Conversely, when an outstanding racemare fails to breed a racehorse in the same class as herself, she is almost invariably dismissed as a bad broodmare. Thus the true picture becomes obscured and wild statements are accepted as fact by many, such as: 'good racemares don't make broodmares' and 'nothing matters in a mare as long as the blood's there', or 'a good line will always come out some time'. Observations of this nature are seldom if ever supported by fact or genetics and should be ignored. One trouble with breeding racehorses is that, like any other enterprise, it requires a great deal of study and experience for anything approaching consistent success to be attained. Sometimes sporadic success arrives through pure luck, but when the luck runs out the breeder is left high and dry unless he possesses a thorough grounding in all facets of the business. Breeders with no real depth of knowledge have succeeded, but apart from luck they have invariably had someone with a true flair and knowledge behind them. An example of this is the late Lord Derby, whose outstanding position as a breeder for many years was due in no small degree to his stud manager Walter Alston, who designed the foundation upon which the stud was built and guided it through the years of its greatest successes.

Thus a breeder without knowledge and experience is well advised, when looking for prospective broodmares, to seek the advice of someone who has proved his ability in this sphere, either as a breeder or adviser.

It is as well for the would-be purchaser not to tie himself down to a mare or filly of any particular category, but to base his choice on the qualities of the individual. If he is starting from scratch, yearling fillies and in-foal mares will give him an immediate racing interest, as opposed to fillies out of training, which are a considerably longer-term policy, especially should they fail to get in foal the first season.

While, as previously noted, bad mares have been known to

breed good racehorses, good racemares have an infinitely better record at stud. The fact than an outstanding racemare may never breed a performer as good as herself does not entitle her to be dismissed as a failure at stud. Outstanding performers are exceptions and nature abhors exceptions. Besides, a limit is set to racing ability by the capacity of a horse's heart, lungs, tendons, etc., despite the great improvement in performance brought about over the years. Thus a breeder must accept the fact that the produce of an exceptional racemare is most unlikely to be in the same class as their dam. In spite of this, they stand a good chance of including racehorses well above the average with further improvement in later generations. Take, for example, two exceptional racemares, Pretty Polly and Sun Chariot, who have often been termed failures at stud.

Pretty Polly (Gallinule–Admiration, by Saraband) was probably the best of her sex to have raced in the present century, winning twenty-two races from twenty-four starts, including the One Thousand Guineas, Oaks, St Leger, Coronation Cup, Champion Stakes and nine two-year-old races, among them the Middle Park Plate, Champagne Stakes, National Breeders' Stakes and Cheveley Park Stakes.

At stud she bred only four winners, but these included the Cheveley Park Stakes winner Molly Desmond, and Polly Flinders, successful in the National Breeders' Stakes, both of whom became good broodmares, as did her non-winning daughters, Dutch Mary and Baby Polly.

Sun Chariot (Hyperion–Clarence, by Diligence) also won the One Thousand Guineas, Oaks and St Leger, as well as proving herself a top-class two-year-old and, like Pretty Polly, superior to the colts of her generation.

At stud, Sun Chariot bred seven winners, of whom Blue Train, Landau and Pindari were in the top class, while Gigantic and Persian Wheel were just below. The daughters of Sun Chariot have not flourished as did those of Pretty Polly as broodmares, but the immediate offspring from Pretty Polly were not so good on the racecourse as those of Sun Chariot.

A mare who achieved brilliance both on the racecourse and at stud was Selene (Chaucer–Serenissima, by Minoru). Bred and raced by the late Lord Derby, Selene won 15½ races, including the Park Hill Stakes, Nassau Stakes and Cheveley Park Stakes.

At stud, Selene gained immortality by breeding Hyperion, as well as Pharamond, Sickle and Hunter's Moon, all top-class horses, and two other winners.

The breeder should always have top-class racing performance in mind before anything else when setting out to buy a brood-mare. If the mare or filly does not possess good racing perform-ance herself, she must be out of a good racemare or, at least, a mare who has produced good racehorses. It is courting fate to buy a mare or filly who has three or four bad mares between herself and the tap-root, as the chances are that any merit attributable to the tap-root has vanished. If a good horse appears from a mare of this category, its ability has come through the sire.

When assessing racing merit, it is important to relate it to opportunity, in the shape of the quality or suitability of the sires in the pedigree and the way in which the individual concerned was trained and exploited on the racecourse. Thus while some racehorses should be better than they are because of their pedigrees, others are better than their pedigrees suggest.

Breeding the best to the best does not necessarily produce the best, since it may result in an imbalance in the pedigree; and in buying a prospective broodmare the breeder should always have at the back of his mind the stallion or stallions with which she is to be mated.

On this principle an over-bred mare who has disappointed on the racecourse may succeed if mated with a tough, unfashion-ably bred stallion, perhaps no more than a good handicapper; whereas a highly bred sire often does best with a roughly bred mare.

Naturally, the choice of a prospective broodmare must depend largely on the buyer's pocket, but it is as well for the latter to have some idea of what he wants before he goes into action.

An in-foal mare who has already produced a winner is a proposition which gives a breeder most to go on. To start with, she has proved she can breed; secondly, she has proved she can breed a winner; next, she has given some idea of the type of stallion which suits her. Apart from assessing her from a veterinary aspect, it does not matter what she looks like if she has produced well-made, sound horses who can win. The crux of the matter is to decide whether the offspring she has produced is better or worse than the mating suggests in the light of the quality and suitability of the sire. If to an apparently excellent mating the mare has produced only a moderate winner, there is little hope of her improving on this. If, on the other hand, she has produced a reasonable winner from an apparently bad mating, there is hope that a more judicious choice of stallion should give a better result. The same argument holds good in buying yearlings. This principle was brought home to me many years ago when Victor Gilpin, to whom I was a pupil at the time, bought a good-looking bay colt by Hurry On out of Pussy Willow, by Polymelus. Though his sire, Hurry On, had sired three Derby winners – Captain Cuttle, Coronach and Call Boy – the Oaks winner Pennycomequick, and Cresta Run, who won the One Thousand Guineas, he was rather out of fashion at that time. The colt's dam, Pussy Willow, had bred a good handicapper by the moderate sire Transcendent (Tracery–Serenity, by Simon Square), so that it was reasonable to hope that Hurry On would show an improvement on Transcendent. Despite this the colt made only 500 guineas in 1930. Named Rolling Rock, he proved a good racehorse, winning the Tattersall Sale Stakes at Doncaster, the Free Handicap from Dastur, to whom he gave 4 lb, and dead-heating with Taj Kasra for the Windsor Castle Stakes at Royal Ascot.

Taking the previously mentioned categories in turn, let us start with a mare already at stud. This subdivides into a mare who has already bred a winner, a mare who has not bred a winner and a barren mare. Two successful cases of the purchase of proven mares are Huntress (Foxhunter–Flapper, by Felstead–Fancy Free) and Sister Sarah (Abbot's Trace–Sarita, by Swynford–Molly Desmond).

Huntress had bred Big Dipper (by Signal Light), the best two-year-old of his year, when she was bought privately by J. J. (now the Hon. Sir John) Astor. Huntress went on to breed eleven winners and though none was in the class of Big Dipper, all were pretty useful, as are a number of her descendants.

Sister Sarah is an example of a mare who maintained the ability to breed good winners when she was well past the age when most mares have retired or are long past their best. Having produced winners including the brilliant two-year-old Lady Sybil and Black Peter, a good horse just below top class, Sister

Sarah was purchased when over 20 by Sir Winston Churchill, for whom she bred Welsh Abbot, one of the best sprinters of his day and a successful sire.

Both Huntress and Sister Sarah had copy-book tail-female lines. Huntress's third dam was Fancy Free, dam of Blue Peter (by Fairway), winner of the Two Thousand, Derby and Eclipse Stakes, while Sister Sarah's grandam was the immortal Pretty Polly.

On the subject of age, as in the human race some mares age more quickly than others and it is advisable to judge the individual on her appearance rather than on her age alone. Old mares are invariably easy to buy, as few breeders want them, and anyone who has not a great deal of money to spend should not necessarily ignore a young-looking old mare of the right qualifications.

One trap to avoid is a bad mare in foal to a good stallion. Any hopes of success are dependent entirely on the stallion and the chances are that, though the offspring might prove a commercial proposition if sold as a yearling, the breeder is left with nothing but a bad mare.

A mare unproven at stud who has not produced a winner must be assessed by the same measure as a yearling or foal. That is to say, her make and shape, the record of her dam on the racecourse and at stud and her pedigree. For instance, when I bought Brazen Molly (Horus–Molly Adare, by Phalaris–Molly Desmond), grandam of Brigadier Gerard, she had not had a runner and was barren, but otherwise her qualifications held water. Owing to the war, she was unbroken, but she was half-sister to several winners, including Fearless Fox (Foxlaw) and Challenge (Apelle), both of whom were high-class winners, and had finished second in the St Leger. Her grandam Molly Desmond (Desmond) won the Cheveley Park Stakes and bred five good winners, among them Spike Island (Spearmint) and Zodiac (Sunstar), each winner of two Irish classics, and Golden Silence (Swynford), who finished second in the Oaks. The next dam was the great racemare and tap-root Pretty Polly. Thus there was an unbroken line of top-class winners and/or producers between Brazen Molly and Pretty Polly. In contrast, some years later I made a purchase which proved injudicious of a mare called Syritha, because she came from the same branch of Pretty Polly.

The flaw in her pedigree was that between Syritha and Molly Adare was a mare, Brave Bird (Flamingo), who was a failure both on the racecourse and at stud, thus breaking the chain of merit in the tail-female line. As a result, Syritha was no good as a broodmare, producing only one moderate winner. Brave Bird, dam of Syritha, was closely related to Brazen Molly, being by Flamingo (by Flamboyant, by Tracery) out of Molly Adare, whereas Brazen Molly was by Horus (by Papyrus, by Tracery) out of Molly Adare. This relationship underlines the fact that pedigree on its own is of little account; it must be closely allied to performance if it is to be given practical significance. As the late George Poole, a successful and eminently practical trainer under both Rules, once observed, 'Every English Thoroughbred is well bred if you're prepared to go far enough back in the pedigree.'

A similar case of a good tap-root being bought cheaply in the shape of an in-foal mare who had neither won nor bred a winner was the purchase of Rosetta (Kantar–Rose Red, by Swynford) by Edgar Cooper-Bland, an astute and highly successful commercial breeder at top level for half a century and responsible for the St Leger winner Bustino (Busted–Ship Yard, by Doutelle), whose third dam is Rosetta.

A failure on the racecourse, Rosetta nevertheless came from a good tail-female line of unbroken winners and producers for several generations. For a commercial breeder she had the added attraction of having been covered by that great racehorse and sire Fairway (Phalaris–Scapa Flow, by Chaucer). The last service was late and there was some doubt as to the mare being in foal – mares were sold untested in those days – but Edgar Cooper-Bland felt sure she was and bought her for a few hundred pounds. His judgement was vindicated to an extent which he can hardly have envisaged, since Rosetta founded a great family which continued to flourish.

While outstanding sires such as Fairway, Pharos, Hyperion and Nearco are usually equally successful as sires of winners or broodmares, there are in any era certain sires who are far better sires of broodmares than they are of winners. These sires fit a definite pattern. Almost invariably they are well-made, good racehorses, with sound rather than high-powered pedigrees, who disappointed as sires of winners. Examples to come to mind are

Straight Deal (Solario–Good Deal, by Apelle), Combat (Big Game–Commotion, by Mieuxce), Vimy (Wild Risk–Mimi, by Black Devil), Worden II (Wild Risk–Sans Tares, by Sind), Mieuxce (Massine–L'Olivete, by Opott), Big Game (Bahram–Myrobella, by Tetratema) and Ratification (Court Martial–Solesa, by Solario).

Straight Deal, who was bred and raced by the late Dorothy Paget and won a wartime Derby, was a good-looking bay horse, having the physical attributes particularly looked for in a broodmare, namely, a deep body with well-sprung ribs and wide quarters, conformation allowing a mare room to hold and deliver a good-sized foal. Straight Deal's tail-female line in the early removes was not particularly aristocratic. His maternal grandsire Apelle (Sardanapale–Angelina, by St Frusquin) had a sound Anglo-French pedigree and was a good racehorse in France, Italy and England, where he won the Coronation Cup, but achieved little as a sire of winners apart from Capiello, a moderate Grand Prix de Paris winner. However, he became the maternal grandsire of Circus Lady (Irish Oaks) and Tenerani (Goodwood Cup, Italian Derby, etc.), as well as of Straight Deal. The sires of the next two dams were the handicapper Arion (Valens), and Rochester (Rock Sand), winner of the Column Produce Stakes and no more than a good handicapper.

Combat, a stable companion and contemporary of the brilliant Tudor Minstrel (Owen Tudor–Sansonnet, by Sansovino), was cleverly placed to go through his racing career unbeaten. He was a good horse, below classic standard and sired only two horses of merit, Aggressor (King George VI and Queen Elizabeth Stakes) and Agar's Plough (Irish Oaks). Combat's dam Commotion (Mieuxce–Riot, by Colorado–Lady Juror) won the Oaks and comes from the great family of Lady Josephine.

It is interesting to note the strong infusion of broodmare sires in the pedigrees of Straight Deal and Combat, since both Apelle, maternal grandsire of Straight Deal, and Mieuxce, maternal grandsire of Combat, were more distinguished as sires of broodmares than as sires of winners.

Vimy, who won the King George VI and Queen Elizabeth Stakes and proved himself a good horse in France, was a well-made individual, otherwise he would not have been acquired by the Irish National Stud, who never buy anything but a truly made stallion. He turned out a disappointing sire of winners, about his best progeny being Khalkis (Eclipse Stakes) and Vimadee (Irish St Leger). As a broodmare sire, Vimy found his mark, the Two Thousand Guineas winner High Top being a notable winner from one of his daughters.

Mieuxce, to whom reference has been made already, was a top-class racehorse in France, where he brought off the rare double of the Prix du Jockey Club (French Derby) and the Grand Prix de Paris. He had an entirely French pedigree and was truly made. Apart from Commotion (Oaks), the best horses by Mieuxce were Paddy's Point, second in the Derby, Feu du Diable (French St Leger) and Stokes (Windsor Castle Stakes, second in the Two Thousand Guineas). Mares by Mieuxce produced winner after winner, among them Crepello, Honeylight and Major Portion.

Ratification had the perfect conformation for a broodmare sire and was a good racehorse with an excellent pedigree. In all he won six races, among them the Coventry Stakes, the Richmond Stakes and the Greenham Stakes, but proved a conspicuous failure as a sire of winners. As a sire of broodmares it is a different story, Sassafras, conqueror of Nijinsky in the Prix de l'Arc de Triomphe, being one of many winners out of a Ratification mare.

One of the reasons why stallions who disappoint as sires of winners succeed as broodmare sires may be because they do not transmit a great deal of nervous energy to their progeny. As a result, when their daughters are mated with highly-bred sires, an imbalance of too much nervous energy is not created.

Typical of the pattern to which so many proven sires of broodmares conform is Royal Palace (Ballymoss–Crystal Palace, by Solar Slipper). A brilliant racehorse, Royal Palace won the Two Thousand Guineas, Derby, Coronation Cup, Eclipse Stakes, King George VI and Queen Elizabeth Stakes, Royal Lodge Stakes and a total of nine races, from two to four years. A disappointing sire of winners, he was a good individual, with powerful quarters and an exceptionally truly formed hind-leg. His ribs were well sprung and he had plenty of heart room, and he has done better as a sire of broodmares.

A filly in or out of training as a prospective broodmare presents the breeder with the information supplied by her racing performance and behaviour in training. This certainly is a help, giving an indication of her racing ability, soundness, temperament, constitution and courage. The more information on these points that the breeder can gain, the better it helps him to assess the possibilities of the filly as a broodmare.

On the whole, at top level, a filly in or out of training who answers the necessary qualifications is a good proposition. She has her whole breeding life before her and the breeder starts with her from scratch, as opposed to a mare who has already gone to stud. Only too often a mare at stud submitted for sale is sent up because there is a snag to her. She may be difficult to get in foal, be a bad mother, have little or no milk, an unpleasant temper, throw bad individuals or have some other drawback. Breeders seldom sell their best mares or an apparently attractive one unless there is a sound reason for parting with her.

It is as well to get a veterinary surgeon to examine a mare or filly, from the breeding aspect, before buying her.

A two-year-old filly has the attraction of the opportunity of racing her. This was the case with Matatina (Grey Sovereign–Zanzara, by Fairey Fulmar), whom Ralph C. Wilson Jr bought at the end of her juvenile season from the late Jack Hylton. For her new owner she proceeded to win the Nunthorpe Stakes, the King George Stakes at Goodwood and the Great St Wilfred Handicap at Ripon, as well as run second in the King's Stand Stakes, July Cup (twice) and the Champion Sprint at Redcar. Matatina had the remarkable record of never being out of the first two in all her fourteen races. At stud she produced several winners, notably New Chapter (Crepello), who beat a good field for the Lincolnshire Handicap and won three other races including the Prix Georges de Kerhallet at Saint-Cloud, and Miss Charisma (Ragusa), a good two-year-old.

In fact, I can think of few good racemares of the right type who failed as broodmares.

English buyers tend to fight shy of mares and fillies sent up for sale at auction by foreign owners, especially if they are not English bred. It is therefore possible, sometimes, to find a bargain in this category. We bought such a filly for our own stud at the December Sales in 1973 for 6,000 guineas, before the market fell, despite her having won a two-year-old race at Saint-Cloud and having been placed in a Group race at three from only a few starts. She had a bad attack of the virus after winning and never recovered her form, so was a better three-year-old than her racing performance indicated. Another factor to militate against her was that her sire Golden Horus (Tudor Melody–Persian Union, by Persian Gulf), died after only one season at stud, so was virtually unknown as a sire, though a good racehorse. Named Gingerale, she was out of Melos, by Hill Gail out of Cyclade, by Djebel; this is a good family developed by Marcel Boussac. She got in foal easily and produced several winners, including Countess Walewski (Brigadier Gerard), winner of her only two races and dam of three winners, two – Cottenham and Croupier – placed in Group races.

Like a filly in training, a yearling filly is an immediate racing proposition, as well as a future broodmare. The late Aga Khan's stud was founded largely upon the judicious purchase of yearling fillies, most famous of these being Mumtaz Mahal (The Tetrarch–Lady Josephine, by Sundridge), Teresina (Tracery–Blue Tit, by Wildfowler) and Cos (Flying Orb–Renaissance, by St Serf).

The Aga Khan selected these three fillies on pedigree, entrusting to the Hon. George Lambton the responsibility of buying them if he approved the conformation.

Mumtaz Mahal was bred by Lady Sykes at the famous Sledmere Stud in Yorkshire. When he set eyes on her, George Lambton made up his mind to buy her. 'I thought her one of the best animals I ever saw in my life,' he remarked. She was knocked down to him in 1920 for 10,000 guineas, a vast sum for those days. Nevertheless Mumtaz Mahal proved a bargain. One of the most brilliantly fast horses of the century, she won five out of her six races as a two-year-old, her single defeat being due to heavy going. She usually won by many lengths and she retained her speed as a three-year-old, when she won the Nunthorpe Stakes, King George Stakes and ran second in the One Thousand Guineas over a distance beyond her best. Mumtaz Mahal proved a succesful broodmare, her winners including Mirza II (Blenheim), a top class two-year-old. Among her daughters were Mah Mahal (Gainsborough), dam of the Derby winner Mahmoud (Blenheim), and Mumtaz Begum (Blenheim), dam of Nasrullah (Nearco).

Whereas Mumtaz Mahal was bred for speed, Teresina, another

product of the Sledmere Stud, had a staying pedigree in the first two removes, although her grandam Petit Bleu was by the sprinter Eager (Enthusiast–Greeba, by Melton). Blue Tit, dam of Teresina, had already bred three winners, of whom Blue Dun (Corcyra) was a good racemare in 1919–21, winning the Phoenix Plate, Manchester November Handicap and over £8,000 in stakes. The Aga Khan paid 7,700 guineas for Teresina and she too proved worth the money, both on the racecourse and at stud.

Throwing to the staying elements in her pedigree, Teresina won the Jockey Club Stakes, Goodwood Cup and two other races, finishing third in the Oaks and in the St Leger and second in the Cesarewitch and the Eclipse Stakes.

As a broodmare, Teresina was more successful than Mumtaz Mahal in that she produced eight winners, among them Theresina (Diophon), Gino (Tetratema), Alishah (Tetratema) and Shahpoor (Solario) all round about top class. Her descendants continued to do well, her daughter Theresina being dam of the St Leger winner Turkhan (Bahram), who finished second in the Derby, and of Ujiji (Umidwar), winner of a wartime Gold Cup and third in the Derby.

Cos was bred by Lord D'Abernon and made 5,000 guineas; like Mumtaz Mahal, she was bred for speed and ran true to her pedigree on the racecourse. A brilliant two-year-old and winner of six races at that age, she ran second in the One Thousand and turned out to be a good broodmare.

Cos bred four winners, all good horses – Costaki Pasha (Gainsborough), Rustom Pasha (Son-in-Law), Mrs Rustom (Blandford) and Hilla (Son-in-Law). Rustom Pasha won the Eclipse and Champion Stakes, later becoming a most successful sire in Argentina. Costaki Pasha won the Middle Park Stakes, Chesham Stakes and Hopeful Stakes from four starts. The family of Cos was successful but not so prolific as that of Mumtaz Mahal or Teresina.

These three fillies are copy-book examples of sound purchases of yearlings likely to be good racers and producers, but they represent rich men's speculations and, provided the buyer has the money to spend, he does not have to be very astute to select them. Their qualifications on breeding are obvious and only their physical aspect calls for any judgement.

I found myself in the agreeable position of having to choose a top-class yearling filly for Jim Joel and had no difficulty in finding one, as her qualifications were there for all to see. This was Rose Dubarry (Klairon–Pristina, by Petition), bred by Sir Kenneth Butt's Brook Stud and whose fifth dam happened to be Mumtaz Mahal. Rose Dubarry's dam Pristina had already bred two good fillies, Mange Tout (Galivanter), winner of the Windsor Castle Stakes, Molecomb Stakes and Prix d'Arenberg, and Hecla (Henry the Seventh), who won the Cherry Hinton Stakes and was placed second in three other races as a two-year-old and at three ran third in the July Cup. Moreover both Galivanter and Henry the Seventh were second-class sires.

Since Klairon had won the French Two Thousand, been narrowly beaten by Our Babu and Tamerlane in the Two Thousand and had proved a most successful sire, whose stock included the Oaks winner Monade, it was reasonable to hope that he would be an improvement on Galivanter and Henry the Seventh. Apart from this, Rose Dubarry was a beautiful individual, only to be faulted in that she was on the small side.

Rose Dubarry cost 30,000 guineas in 1970 and established herself as the best two-year-old filly of her year, being unbeaten in her three starts, including the Lowther Stakes and the Norfolk Stakes (now the Flying Childers Stakes); at three she finished third in the One Thousand Guineas. She disappointed at stud, but bred two winners.

It will be seen that two of the Aga Khan's three fillies mentioned were bred for speed and one for stamina.

On the whole, a fast mare is probably a better proposition as a producer than a stayer, but whether a sprinter or a stayer, one type should be avoided – the one-pacer. An essential quality in a racehorse is the ability to quicken; this enables him to take a position in a race, make use of fleeting openings and produce an effective finishing run. The one-pacer has to be good enough to go from start to finish and grind the opposition into the ground, for he cannot vary his tactics. This places him at a tactical disadvantage, since it is easier to ride, or run, a race from behind than from the front and gives little scope for saving a horse. Thus a stayer with good acceleration is a better proposition than a one-paced sprinter or miler as a prospective broodmare, always provided she answers the other necessary qualifications and is properly mated.

Not every breeder is in the position to find a great deal of money for a yearling, filly or broodmare. Those not so happily placed must cast their net more widely and less ambitiously. They will have to sacrifice something, be it pedigree, racing performance, temperament, constitution or conformation, and must look beyond the obvious.

To my mind, pedigree is the first quality to sacrifice, since pedigree is a guide and not a guarantee. This does not mean buying fluke-bred animals, but being prepared to take a chance with unfashionable names in otherwise sound pedigrees.

This aspect was first brought home to me through the success of Roderic More O'Ferrall of the Kildangan Stud, responsible for half a dozen classic winners since the war. The principle upon which he worked was to seek out mares or fillies from families which had consistently done far better on the racecourse than their breeding suggested, and upgrade them through the use of top-class stallions. The prime example is Laitron (Solden-nis–Chardon, by Aldford), which by top standards is plebeian breeding. Mated with On Parade, Almaska, Rosewell and Sol Oriens, all far removed from classic sires, Laitron produced winners. She was then acquired by Roderic More O'Ferrall and mated with Denturius and Nearco; better class winners in Dairymaid and Nella emerged. The next generation stepped straight into the classic sphere; Dairymaid bred the One Thousand Guineas winner Abermaid, while Nella was the dam of Miralgo, who ran third in the St Leger, won the Hardwicke Stakes, Timeform Gold Cup and other races. Both mares produced good winners besides Abermaid and Miralgo.

Taking a leaf out of Roderic More O'Ferrall's notebook, in 1965 I bought for 700 guineas a grey filly by Arctic Time (Arctic Star–Dancing Time, by Colombo) out of Mrs Dale, by Impeccable. This is hardly a pedigree to inspire the fashion-conscious, but the tail-female line had consistently produced winners to moderate sires and Mrs Dale herself had proved a good racemare at two, three and four years, also having produced several winners. Named Bell Crofts – readers of Trollope will appreciate the choice – the filly won and was placed, in spite of being struck down by a severe attack of the virus. Her first foal, Eleanor Bold (Queen's Hussar), won and was placed as a two-year-old; her second foal died before he raced; her third, Posy

(Major Portion), won as a two-year-old, beating a very useful filly in Be Tuneful, and at three finished second in the Nell Gwyn Stakes and led the field in the One Thousand Guineas till a furlong and a half from home, eventually finishing ninth; she also ran third in the Marlborough House Stakes at Ascot. The fourth foal, Lizzie Eustace (Firestreak), won several races.

An odd coincidence is that three of Bell Croft's foals were dropped on 7 April.

Thus, though not having reached the status of Laitron as a foundation mare, Bell Crofts justified her purchase.

The purchase of a filly foal as a prospective broodmare is a fairly long-term policy, but as such it sometimes enables the buyer to acquire her at a relatively lower price than if she were a yearling. The principles of her purchase are the same as those for buying a yearling.

In buying either a foal or a yearling, it is a mistake to judge them in the same light as one would judge a horse in training. Foals or yearlings who look as if they are small racehorses seldom come up to expectations, because they are too set and have little scope for development or improvement.

Two types who often fail on the racecourse but succeed at stud are twins and closely inbred mares, so bargains can be sought in each category.

Though a twin may be undersized, this is a physical state due to the fact of being a twin, and not one due to heredity. Thus there is every chance of her producing normal-sized foals. One of the most famous twins among broodmares is Lady Bawn (Le Noir–Milady, by Kisber), dam of five winners including Bachelor's Double, all of them being by Tredennis.

Another example is the twins Orum Blaze and Orum Star, by Umidwar–Gold Race, by Colorado, who made a name for themselves. Both were nice fillies, not unduly small, and each bred four winners, Orum Blaze winning a good-class race herself. Orum Blaze was the better broodmare and bred two very useful horses in Prince d'Or and Prince Fortune, both by Prince Chevalier.

The dam of Orum Blaze and Orum Star, Gold Race, is a good example of a bad, ugly racemare with a good pedigree turning out to be a successful broodmare.

Gold Race, who was bred by Lt-Col. Giles Loder, was a black, coffin-headed, highly nervous filly, rather straight in front and in the shoulder. It was my lot sometimes to hack her out with the string in an endeavour to calm her down. She was a kind, gentle filly but the treatment made no difference to her racing ability, since she did nothing on the racecourse.

Gold Race had a superb pedigree; her sire Colorado was top class on the racecourse and at stud, unfortunately dying young, and her dam Cresta Run won the One Thousand Guineas.

Cresta Run bred only two winners, neither of any consequence, but like a number of good racehorses passed on her ability through a daughter, Gold Race, who besides being the dam of Orum Blaze and Orum Star produced Gold Nib (Dastur), a good miler who ran third in the Two Thousand and became a successful sire in New Zealand, and a useful sprinter in Goldhill (Sir Cosmo).

One of the best examples of a good, inbred broodmare is Flagette (see pedigree on p. 105), dam of the top-class French racehorse and sire in the USA Herbager (Vandale). Flagette is by Escamillo by Firdaussi, out of Fidgette, by Firdaussi.

Though not the dam of so distinguished a horse as Herbager, the still more closely inbred Double Strength (Umidwar–Umigal, by Umidwar) both bred a winner and possessed a measure of racing ability despite not actually winning. Double Strength was bred by the late Sir Rhys Llewellyn, the writer on breeding and genetics and author of *Breeding to Race*.

One reason for inbred mares often proving successful at stud is that they offer scope and contrast when they come to be mated.

The choice of a broodmare from a general aspect is a personal matter. Some breeders do not care what a mare looks like so long as she breeds winners, nor do they care what her offspring look like so long as they win races.

Winning races is the object of the exercise, so that there is practical sense in this philosophy. Nevertheless, it is much more agreeable to look out upon handsome mares than on ugly ones and, on the whole, good racehorses have good conformation. Even if the precept of one old-time stud manager – 'Never buy a mare that wouldn't win in the show ring' – may be carrying perfection too far, it is not a bad measure to have at the back of one's mind.

An aspect of conformation that must be considered is the fact that certain faults of conformation tend to go with certain sires and broodmares. For instance, horses by Phalaris tended to be back at the knee, those by Tourbillon to have their hocks away from them. In such cases it is advisable to overlook these drawbacks, since the racing ability of the individual may go with them, but try to correct them when they come to be mated.

The late Dick Dawson, who trained so many of the late Aga Khan's best horses, once remarked, 'I can't abide a perfect horse,' and on his patron's instructions most unwillingly bid for and secured a faultless yearling which proved useless.

Several good judges, among them Fred Darling, have told me: 'Look at a horse's head first, as it will give an indication of his character; then start at his feet and work upwards.' If a horse has a mean, ungenerous-looking head, with a small eye and cunning expression, he or she is best avoided, no matter how taking the rest of the conformation may be.

Faults of conformation must be weighed against other factors and an assessment be made accordingly. For instance, the late Peter McCall, one of the ablest stud managers in the business and a successful breeder on his own account, selected a yearling filly for the Someries Stud to race and eventually make a broodmare. She was a beautiful individual with a superb pedigree, but had one fault – curbs. These were not pronounced and were on good, strong hocks. Rightly, Peter McCall judged that the curbs would in no way affect the filly's racing performance and bought her. She turned out to be Roussalka (Habitat–Oh So Fair, by Graustark), who traces in tail-female to Mumtaz Mahal, was a brilliant two-year-old, one of the best three-year-old fillies of her year, and has proved a good broodmare. Had the curbs been on weak hocks, or accompanied by any serious flaw, it would have been another matter.

When considering the purchase of a mare or filly unproven at stud, but who has racing performance, it is important to evalutate the form carefully. A winner has not necessarily more to recommend her than a non-winner, since the quality of the performance might be inferior in the case of the winner to that of the non-winner.

5

Choice of a Stallion

When, on looking through past records, a breeder sees the number of useless racehorses who are full brothers or sisters to classic winners, he may well wonder whether there is anything in mating horses at all. And as some of the best racehorses in Turf history have been bred by pure chance, Pretty Polly for one, Alycidon for another – the stallion to whom his dam was going died suddenly and since it was wartime and Donatello II happened to be standing at the same stud, the mare was covered by him – the breeder cannot be blamed for putting the whole business down to luck, placing the names of his mares in one hat, those of the stallions available in another and arranging the matings according to the order in which the names come out.

Though this method might be entertaining, and even produce a good racehorse, it would entail much wastage. On the other side of the coin, a successful mating repeated has often produced other excellent results, for example that of Phalaris and Scapa Flow, respectively sire and dam of Fairway (St Leger, etc.), Fair Isle (One Thousand Guineas) and Pharos (Champion Stakes, etc., second in the Derby).

While the genetic pattern of the individual cannot be predicted with anything approaching certainty, a well-balanced, intelligently conceived mating stands a better chance of succeeding than a badly balanced and ill-conceived one.

It is virtually impossible for the owner of a large number of mares to mate each one exactly as he wishes. Circumstances such as late-foaling mares, mares who are difficult to foal, those who travel badly, etc., all serve to complicate the operation, so that the breeder perforce has to give his choicest mares preferential treatment and mate the others as best he can, often not to their fullest advantage.

One good reason for attempting to avoid faults of conformation, soundness, temperament and constitution in both mares and stallions is that it helps to simplify the problems of mating. Even when the greatest trouble is taken, the results may be disappointing, and vice versa. I once mated a mare who was back at the knee with a stallion having the same fault and got a foal with a perfect foreleg: it proved a bad racehorse, perhaps because it inherited neither the faults nor racing ability. Nevertheless, when strict attention is paid to make and shape and all other important factors the chances of failure are somewhat lessened.

Before embarking on the mating of his mares, the breeder should have available as much information as possible about his mares and the stallions he proposes to use. That is to say, knowledge of their conformation, soundness, temperament, racing ability, constitution, behaviour in training, appetite and, most important, whether they have been treated with hormones, anabolic steroids or dope. Not unnaturally, some of this information is not always available, sometimes because breeders make little attempt to acquire it, especially in respect of stallions being syndicated, as it were, at gun-point: 'We must have your reply at once,' concerning the offer of a share in a stallion, perhaps a foreign horse of which the breeder has no knowledge except of his racing record which, being foreign, may mean little.

For this situation breeders have no one but themselves to blame. If they were all more particular about knowing everything about a stallion before taking a share in him, they would have fewer failures and waste less money.

The distasteful fact has to be faced that few horses make top-class stallions and the average racehorse bred is not much good. Even if a horse turns out to be a top stallion, there is often a chance to acquire a share or a nomination to him later on, either by an exchange of nominations or by buying a share or nomination when he is temporarily out of favour, or through death or a dispersal sale. On this principle it is better to chance missing the bus than be bustled into an expensive share in or nomination to an unproven horse, concerning which there may not be full information.

When a racehorse hits the headlines there is invariably a rush to buy shares in him, regardless of the true nature of his qualifications. To start with, the mere fact that he wins a number of top races does not mean, necessarily, that he is a champion. He may be a good horse in a bad year and if he is

retired before he had completed a competitive four-year-old
season it is even more difficult to assess his correct merit. A
typical instance was Tulyar's (Tehran–Neocracy, by Nearco).
Though on the face of it Tulyar's form read well, in fact he was
over-rated as a racehorse and had he remained in training as a
four-year-old undoubtedly would have been 'found out'. Raced
as a four-year-old, Tulyar would have had to take on Pinza and
Aureole, both in my opinion markedly superior to him.

While racing performance is no guarantee to success at stud,
it is important to know exactly how good a horse really was.
Besides, when a horse is retired to stud on an inflated reputation,
breeders using him are paying an inflated price.

There is no doubt that in most cases the owner of a horse
who had acquired a reputation beyond his actual merit nearly
always comes off best financially if he can syndicate him before
there is any chance of the bubble bursting. It is worth noting
that the late Aga Khan, a shrewd business man, retired all his
Derby winners – Blenheim, Bahram, Mahmoud, My Love and
Tulyar – at the end of their three-year-old season. Of these
Derby winners only Bahram seemed likely to stand a chance of
enhancing his reputation by being trained as a four-year-old,
since he was undoubtedly a really good horse, who suffered
through being unable to show his true ability because of the
poor quality of his opponents.

When a horse comes into the limelight through a series of
important victories, it is often a better proposition to use his
sire than to pay an exaggerated price for a share in the horse
himself, since the pattern of mating which produced the good
racehorse is there for the breeder to see and can be repeated. For
instance, after the successes of Grundy (Great Nephew–Word
from Lundy, by Worden II), I had no difficulty in acquiring a
nomination to Great Nephew for a comparatively modest sum.
Grundy's pedigree indicated that Great Nephew was best suited
to a tough, outcross mare rather than a highly-bred mare and he
had shown that he could sire winners. Grundy, on the other
hand, was unproven as a four-year-old, expensive and an
unknown quantity at stud, where he achieved little.

This does not mean that a breeder should not take a chance
on an unproven stallion, but that he should go into the project
with care, and unless money is of no object, try to obtain value.

The fewer mares a breeder has in his stud, the more discriminating he can be, so that before buying a share in or taking a nomination to a stallion he will have in mind the mare for which he will use it. Once a breeder decides that he wants to use a stallion, he should give him a fair trial before discarding him. Stallions can take some time to get going and to indicate the type of mare best suited to them, so a breeder must be prepared for failures before he hits on the right mating. Many stallions disappoint because they seldom get the type of mare to which they are most suited.

As remarked previously, some stallions prove failures as sires of winners but do well as sires of broodmares. On this basis, a nice mare by a stallion who has not come up to expectations as a sire of winners should not be culled in too great a hurry if she fails on the racecourse. I would think twice about getting rid of a nice mare by Royal Palace, even if she proved a bad racemare.

Many breeders are prejudiced against old stallions. Unless the horse has poor fertility, this bias has no scientific foundation and, in fact, stallions sometimes sire their best son or daughter in their last season at stud. One to do so was Donatello II (Blenheim–Delleana, by Clarissimus), who got Crepello in the final year of his life.

As in a prospective broodmare, acceleration is a more important attribute in a stallion than one-paced speed.

Between the two wars the breeder with classic ambitions had an easier task than his counterpart today. During that era there were a number of middle-distance stallions of classic calibre who consistently sired horses of top racing ability; such stallions were Phalaris, Blandford, Pharos, Gainsborough and Hurry On. While, obviously, there were many bad horses sired by these stallions, they got a remarkably high percentage of top-class horses and most of the classic winners in that era had one of them as his or her sire. Besides, breeding was more insular, only a few American horses coming to race or stand at stud here.

The trend continued with Hyperion (Gainsborough–Selene, by Chaucer) and Nearco (Pharos–Nogara, by Havresac II), then came the tendency for classic winners to be by different sires, to be followed by the overwhelming influence of Northern Dancer.

Consistency in the post-war era was more evident among sires of sprinters and milers, such as Court Martial (Fair Trial–Instantaneous, by Hurry On), Grey Sovereign (Nasrullah–Kong, by Baytown) and Fair Trial (Fairway–Lady Juror, by Son-in-Law), and later by the male line of Sing Sing (Tudor Minstrel–Agin the Law, by Portlaw) and Habitat (Sir Gaylord–Little Hut, by Occupy). This is understandable to a certain extent, since the sprinter-cum-miler is concerned almost solely with speed, whereas the top middle-distance classic horse needs the speed of a sprinter and the ability to get one and a half miles in the highest class.

An interesting aspect of other successful sires of top-class middle-distance winners is that a number were not mile-and-a-half horses, for instance Hard Sauce (Ardan–Saucy Bella, by Bellacose), sire of Hard Ridden, Never Bend (Nasrullah–Lalun, by Djeddah), sire of Mill Reef, and Queen's Hussar (March Past–Jojo, by Vilmorin), sire of Brigadier Gerard and Highclere, whereas before the war, except for Phalaris (Polymelus–Bromus, by Sainfoin), who was a miler, it was the mile-and-a-half plus horse – the winner of the St Leger rather than a Derby winner – who usually sired the winner of the Derby, such as Blandford, Hyperion, Fairway and Hurry On.

Speed and stamina are qualities which are not easy to pin down because in the case of a really good horse it is sometimes difficult to assess exactly his best distance. After Brigadier Gerard had won the King George VI and Queen Elizabeth Stakes, Alec Head remarked: 'With horses like Brigadier Gerard distance makes no difference.'

When viewing sires from the point of view of speed, it is as well to bear in mind that the champion sprinter is not always the fastest horse of his generation, because the latter may be one who is being exploited over further distances. Tommy Weston once told me that Fairway was the fastest horse he had ever ridden, but his brilliance as a sprinter was obscured by this successes over middle distances and further. Likewise, had he been exploited over sprint distances, Brigadier Gerard would have beaten the best sprinters of his day.

Professional sprint stallions, such as Gold Bridge, Sir Cosmo, Panorama and Vilmorin, are valuable assests in a pedigree, because they introduce fine physique as well as pure speed, but they seldom sire, or produce through their daughters, a really good horse over a mile and a half in the first generation. The tendency is for the progeny to excel short of twelve furlongs or beyond twelve furlongs. Interesting examples of this principle are the cases of Rustom Pasha (Son-in-Law–Cos, by Flying Orb) and Epigram (Son-in-Law–Flying Sally, by Flying Orb). Rustom Pasha's best distance was eight to ten furlongs, while Epigram excelled over two miles. The professional sprinter – that is to say the horse evolved from dominant sprinting sires, such as The Boss (Orby–Southern Cross II, by Meteor) – is distinct from the 'classic' sprinter, such as Tetratema (The Tetrarch–Scotch Gift, by Symington), Abernant (Owen Tudor–Rustom Mahal, by Rustom Pasha) and Friar Marcus (Cicero–Prim Nun, by Persimmon). Such horses are bred to stay ten to twelve furlongs, but do not do so, their racing merit being essentially in speed. These sometimes produce a top mile-and-a-half horse through one of their daughters – for instance, Friar Marcus, maternal grandsire of Bahram. They are more predictable influences in a middle-distance classic pedigree than the professional sprinter and on a short-term policy mares by them are a better proposition for a breeder with classic ambitions than are mares by professional sprinting sires.

The unpredictable nature of inheritance in the Thoroughbred makes it virtually impossible to foretell the merit of an unproven stallion. A case in point is the contrasting success at stud of the Derby and Two Thousand Guineas winner Nimbus (Nearco–Kong, by Baytown) and his half brother, Grey Sovereign (Nasrullah–Kong, by Baytown): Nimbus was a disappointing sire, Grey Sovereign a good one.

One successful guess I was fortunate enough to make about an unproven sire was the choice of Queen's Hussar, sire of Brigadier Gerard and Highclere. Had I been more affluent at the time, I might well have overlooked Queen's Hussar through casting my net in more expensive waters. As it was, my search was concentrated in the area of stallions standing at not more than £500. Queen's Hussar came well within this figure as he stood then at only £250. Had Brigadier Gerard been the only classic winner, or horse of comparable ability, to be sired by Queen's Hussar, it is arguable that his feat in getting the Brigadier was a genetic fluke, but when he sired a One Thousand

Guineas and French Oaks winner in Highclere, as well as a steady flow of lesser winners, it became evident that this was not so. Another lucky choice was Night Shift (Northern Dancer–Ciboulette, by Chop Chop), based on his conformation, character, action, pedigree and that, owing to an operation on his throat – not for wind infirmity – going wrong, his racing merit was greater than his form showed.

The success of Brigadier Gerard and Highclere underlines the advantage held by private breeders over commercial breeders, in that the former have only themselves to please and can use cheap, unfashionable stallions if they wish to do so, whereas the commercial breeder must always think of the market.

For the private breeder, the most important aspect of choosing a stallion is the suitability of the horse to the mare. This being the case, the first step of the breeder is to study carefully every character of his mares and upon the result choose a stallion for each, rather than lumbering himself with a number of shares and nominations without thought as to how he is going to use them.

An important point about judging a stallion's conformation and physical characters is that he must be assessed according to what he was as a horse in training, not as he is at stud, because his offspring, if they inherit his characters as a racehorse, will resemble him at that stage, not as he is as a stallion.

In modern times about the most successful international stallion has been Nasrullah (Nearco–Mumtaz Begum, by Blenheim–Mumtaz Mahal). He was a brilliant, but temperamental racehorse and highly bred. When a high-powered pedigree gets away with it, that is to say, produces a horse in which brilliance is achieved without temperamental imbalance (or the other extreme of complete lack of brilliance or temperament, in other words a useless racehorse), the product often excels both on the racecourse and at stud. Hyperion is one example, Nasrullah another and, to a lesser degree, Royal Charger a third. At the same time, on the principle that you can seldom have the jam without the powder, such a pedigree often proves a two-edged sword as regards temperament. 'I've had some brilliant Nearcos but I sometimes never want to see another in the yard,' Frank Butters once remarked under the burden of the tantrums of Nasrullah and Masaka (Nearco–Majideh, by Mahmoud), though the former won him the Coventry Stakes and the Champion Stakes and the latter the Oaks, Irish Oaks and Queen Mary Stakes.

Nevertheless, brilliance is the essence of championship performance on the racecourse and, rather than lose it, the breeder must do all in his power to counterbalance and retain it. Otherwise he may well go through life breeding handicappers.

It is not an easy task to achieve a happy balance between temperament and brilliance, as the temperament of so many of the best offspring of Hyperion show – Sun Chariot, Godiva and Aureole are three instances. But it is not impossible, as instanced by the good but placid Owen Tudor (ex Mary Tudor, by Pharos–Anna Bolena, by Teddy), winner of the Derby and a wartime Gold Cup. Likewise, Nasrullah sired many good horses of equable temperament, such as the Two Thousand Guineas winner Nearula (ex Respite, by Flag of Truce) and the Derby and St Leger winner Never Say Die (ex Singing Grass, by War Admiral).

In such cases there is usually a strong counterbalancing outcross close up in the pedigree: Teddy (Ajax–Rondeau, by Bay Ronald) in the case of Owen Tudor, Flag of Truce (Truculent–Concordia, by Son-in-Law) in that of Nearula and War Admiral (Man o'War–Brush Up, by Sweep) with Never Say Die.

Every now and then a good racehorse emerges with a plebeian pedigree, or one with indifferent representatives close up in it. In most cases these horses fail, or at least disappoint, as sires. Examples are Trigo and Windsor Lad, both by the outstanding sire Blandford, but 'roughly' bred on the dams' side, Trigo being out of a mare by Farasi and Windsor Lad from a daughter of By George!, stallions of little consequence.

However, if a horse proves able to sire racehorses of merit, despite flaws in his pedigree, this factor can be ignored: as in racing it is performance that counts, not pedigree. A striking example is Shirley Heights (Mill Reef–Hardiemma, by Hardicanute), whose dam's pedigree is far from aristocratic but has not prevented him from siring top-class horses, among them the Derby winner Slip Anchor. A similar sire from earlier times is Hurry On, by the handicapper Marcovil and sire of the Derby winners Captain Cuttle, Coronach and Call Boy.

6

Mating of Mares

While the result of a mating is not predictable to any exactitude, a breeder should at least know what he is trying to produce: a sprinter, stayer, middle-distance horse, classic horse, two-year-old winner, a general purpose horse or a jumper. At various times I have been asked for advice on matings and sometimes the breeder in question has no idea as to what type of horse he wants to breed or what he intends to do with it when it is foaled. It is difficult enough to succeed with a clear plan in mind; to have no plan leads to chaos.

There are so many aspects of mating Thoroughbred horses that it is difficult to know where to start when attacking the problem. On the principle that top middle-distance racing ability is the aim of every ambitious breeder, it seems reasonable to begin by analysing the pedigrees of some of the outstanding performers in this category to have raced after the 1914–18 war.

While there is always much controversy concerning the merits of top horses, few will dispute the outstanding merit of the following half-dozen: Fairway (1925), Hyperion (1930), Bahram (1932), Ribot (1952), Nijinsky (1967) and Brigadier Gerard (1968). These therefore are chosen as subjects of this analysis.

Fairway was bred by the late Lord Derby and trained at Newmarket by Frank Butters. The Hon. George Lambton was Lord Derby's racing manager at that time and wrote of Fairway:

> When he came into training he was still a light-framed leggy customer, but from the very beginning of his active work neither I nor his trainer, Frank Butters, had the slightest doubt as to his being a colt of the very first class. He had beautiful shoulders and the best set of legs and feet that I have ever seen on a racehorse – hard ground or soft came alike to him – and, added to other qualities, the bloodlike intelligent head of the highclass Thoroughbred. He was not in any way like his sire Phalaris, and took after his grandsire Polymelus; but, like most of the stock of

FAIRWAY
b. 1925

Phalaris, br. 1913				
Polymelus	Cyllene	Bona Vista	Bend Or	
			Vista	
		Arcadia	Isonomy	
			Distant Shore	
	Maid Marian	Hampton	Lord Clifden	
			Lady Langden	
		Quiver	Toxophilite	
			D. of Y. Melbourne	
Bromus	Sainfoin	SPRINGFIELD	St Albans	
			Viridis	
		Sanda	Wenlock	
			Sandal	
	Cheery	ST SIMON	Galopin	
			St Angela	
		Sunrise	SPRINGFIELD	
			Sunray	

Scapa Flow, ch. 1914				
Chaucer	ST SIMON	Galopin	Vedette	
			Flying Duchess	
		St Angela	King Tom	
			Adeline	
	Canterbury Pilgrim	Tristan	HERMIT	
			Thrift	
		Pilgrimage	The Earl or The Palmer	
			Lady Audley	
Anchora	Love Wisely	Wisdom	Blinkhoolie	
			Aline	
		Lovelorn	Philammon	
			Gone	
	Eryholme	Hazlehatch	HERMIT	
			Hazeldean	
		Ayrsmoss	Ayrshire	
			Battlewings	

Phalaris, he was inclined to be nervous and fretful when first put into fast work.

Fairway certainly lived up to the high opinion which George Lambton and Frank Butters formed of him. He proved an outstanding racehorse from five furlongs to 2½ miles, winning twelve races from fifteen starts at two, three and four years, including the St Leger, Champion Stakes and Jockey Club Stakes. His only defeats were when unplaced in his first race, in the Derby, when he became extremely overwrought in the preliminaries, and when beaten by Royal Minstrel (Tetratema-Harpischord, by Louvois) in his second Eclipse Stakes.

Fairway proved a highly successful sire, heading the list four times.

The first point about Fairway's pedigree to strike the eye is the 3×4 inbreeding to St Simon. This undoubtedly was a factor in Fairway's ability as a racehorse.

Fairway's sire Phalaris, though impeccably bred, was no more than a good handicapper who only stayed a mile, but he proved in the top class as a sire.

Scapa Flow, dam of Fairway, was a handicapper, one of her victories being in a selling plate. She had a stout rather than distinguished pedigree; her sire Chaucer ran for five seasons, was a good two-year-old and a top-class middle-distance handicapper in later life. Anchora, grandam of Fairway, won eight races from fifty starts in second-class, staying company. Her sire, Love Wisely, was an incredibly tough horse of whom his trainer Alec Taylor, a man not given to being easy in his methods, remarked that he was the stoutest horse he had ever trained.

Fairway's tail-female line was sound rather than distinguished, producing useful winners such as The Owl (Wisdom), winner of the Newmarket Stakes; but it is not until we come to Fairway's sixth dam Mavis (Macaroni), who bred the Two Thousand Guineas winner Galliard (Galopin), that a classic winner is to be found and this is too far back to be of more than academic interest.

Thus the pattern of the pedigree can be summed up as: the high-powered ability of St Simon, together with the speed and nervous energy of Phalaris, counterbalanced by the tough, sober, staying qualities introduced through Fairway's dam Scapa Flow and grandam Anchora, the latter's sire, Love Wisely, and Chaucer's maternal grandsire, Tristan, a horse of iron who won the Ascot Gold Cup, three Champion Stakes, three Hardwicke Stakes and innumerable other races.

Hyperion, who like Fairway was bred and owned by the late Lord Derby, shows in his pedigree exactly the same inbreeding to St Simon as Fairway. This pedigree is also an example of brilliance counterbalanced by stout, steadying influences, but these qualities are differently arranged from those in the pedigree of Fairway.

As opposed to Fairway's sire, Phalaris, who was a miler and inclined to sire excitable stock, Hyperion's sire, Gainsborough, was a stout, sober horse of top classic ability and stamina, which he passed on to many of his sons and daughters. Gainsborough won the Autumn Stakes as a two-year-old, the triple crown and a substitute Ascot Gold Cup, all his racing having taken place during the war. His sire, Bayardo, was one of the best horses to race in this century, winning in the top class at

HYPERION
ch. 1930

Gainsborough, b. 1915	Bayardo	Bay Ronald	Hampton	Lord Clifden
				Lady Langden
			Black Duchess	Galliard
				Black Corrie
		Galicia	GALOPIN	Vedette
				Flying Duchess
			Isoletta	Isonomy
				Lady Muncaster
	Rosedrop	St Frusquin	ST SIMON	GALOPIN
				St Angela
			Isabel	Plebian
				Parma
		Rosaline	Trenton	Musket
				Frailty
			Rosalys	Bend Or
				Rosa May
Selene, b. 1919	Chaucer	ST SIMON	GALOPIN	Vedette
				Flying Duchess
			St Angela	King Tom
				Adeline
		Canterbury Pilgrim	Tristan	Hermit
				Thrift
			PILGRIMAGE	The Earl or The Palmer
				Lady Audley
	Serenissima	Minoru	Cyllene	Bona Vista
				Arcadia
			Mother Siegel	Friar's Balsam
				Dau. of Galopin
		Gondolette	Loved One	See Saw
				PILGRIMAGE
			Dongola	Doncaster
				Douranee

all distances. Gainsborough's dam, Rosedrop, won the Oaks. Like Fairway, Hyperion was out of a mare by Chaucer, but his tail-female line was far more distinguished than Fairway's. Selene, dam of Hyperion, was a really good racemare and broodmare; she won seven races as a two-year-old, among them the Cheveley Park Stakes, adding another seven and a dead-heat to her score the following season, including the Park Hill Stakes and the Nassau Stakes. At stud Selene bred ten winners, of whom besides Hyperion, Sickle (Phalaris), Pharamond (Phalaris) and Hunter's Moon (Hurry On) were of classic calibre.

Hyperion's grandam, Serenissima, won twice in second-class company and bred eight winners including Tranquil (Swynford), who won the One Thousand Guineas and St Leger, and the Ascot Gold Cup winner Bosworth (Son-in-Law). The next dam, Gondolette, produced the Derby winner Sansovino, Ferry who won the One Thousand Guineas, both by Swynford, and eight other winners.

It is difficult to visualize a more perfect, classic pedigree than that of Hyperion, who lived up to it by winning the Derby, St

BAHRAM
b. 1932

Blandford, b. 1915	Swynford	John o' Gaunt	Isinglass	**ISONOMY** / Deadlock
			La Fleche	**ST SIMON** / Quiver
		Canterbury Pilgrim	Tristan	Hermit / Thrift
			Pilgrimage	The Earl or The Palmer / Lady Audley
	Blanche	White Eagle	Gallinule	**ISONOMY** / Moorhen
			Merry Gal	Galopin / Mary Seaton
		Black Cherry	Hendigo	Ben Battle / Hasty Girl
			Black Duchess	Galliard / Black Corrie
Friar's Daughter, br. 1921	Friar Marcus	Cicero	Cyllene	Bona Vista / Arcadia
			Gas	Ayrshire / Illuminata
		Prim Nun	Persimmon	**ST SIMON** / Perdita II
			Nonsuch	Nunthorpe / La Morlaye
	Garron Lass	Roseland	William the Third	**ST SIMON** / Gravity
			Electric Rose	Lesterlin / Arc Light
		Concertina	**ST SIMON**	Galopin / St Angela
			Comic Song	Petrarch / Frivolity

Leger, New Stakes at Ascot, Dewhurst Stakes, etc. and headed the list of winning sires six times.

Hyperion was small in height, so small as a yearling that he nearly was not trained at all, but was a beautiful mover so it was decided to give him a chance. He was well made, with good shoulders, excellent limbs, strong quarters and a particularly good hind leg. His appearance was only to be faulted in that the set of his head and neck was not attractive.

While Fairway was a better, faster racehorse than Hyperion, the latter proved the more successful sire.

Bahram, who was bred and raced by the late Aga Khan, I always thought to be the best racehorse I saw in action before the war – I saw Fairway only at stud – and Frank Butters, who trained both Bahram and Fairway, rated the former the better of the two, though Bill Freeman, the travelling lead-lad, once told me that he rated Fairway superior; it is possible that Fairway gave this impression through being a more spectacular worker at home.

As noted earlier, Bahram's reputation suffered from the fact that his path was cast in easy lines: he raced in a year of moderate horses, never took on older horses and did not race as a four-year-old. Yet the ease and immaculate style of his victories, his performance in the St Leger and Butters's opinion convince me that Bahram was a great horse. Bahram was never beaten. He won all his five races as a two-year-old – the National Breeders' Stakes, the Rous Memorial Stakes (Goodwood), Gimcrack Stakes, Boscawen Stakes and Middle Park Stakes. At three he won the triple crown and St James's Palace Stakes. When winning the St Leger, in a fraction over record time, Bahram was being virtually pulled up in the last furlong. Had he been sent along to the winning post, he would have shattered the record. This emphasises that time records in England must be taken with a pinch of salt.

Bahram was a beautifully balanced horse of the highest quality, almost impossible to fault, with a perfect temperament and superb action. His one weakness was that, like most of the stock of Blandford, he disliked heavy going, in which conditions he put up the one unimpressive performance of his career, in the St James's Palace Stakes.

Bahram's stud career was disrupted by his premature export to the USA at the beginning of the war, but through his sons Big Game (ex Myrobella, by Tetratema), Persian Gulf (ex Double Life, by Bachelor's Double) and Turkhan (ex Theresina, by Diophon), as well as a number of his daughters, such as Doubleton (ex Daily Double, by Fair Trial), grandam of Meld, Mah Iran (ex Mah Mahal, by Gainsborough), dam of Migoli and grandam of Petite Etoile, and Queen of Baghdad (ex Queen of Scots, by Dark Legend), dam of Noor, he has become an important name in Thoroughbred breeding.

The general pattern of Bahram's pedigree can be described as the reverse of Fairway's, in that Bahram was by a sire with stamina on a fast-bred mare. His sire, Blandford, one of the great sires of the century, was a racehorse of classic ability who suffered from having no classic engagements owing to an injury incurred as a yearling.

Friar's Daughter, dam of Bahram, cost Bahram's owner-breeder, the late Aga Khan, only 250 guineas as a yearling. She won and was second four times as a two-year-old, proving herself a sound, genuine, consistent performer, some way below top class.

Bahram's grandam Garron Lass never raced and bred only two foals. The next dam, Concertina, was a great tap-root, being the dam of Plucky Liege, who produced Sir Gallahad III, Bull Dog, Admiral Drake, Bois Roussel, etc.

Thus, like Hyperion, Bahram came from a classic tail-female line.

Though showing no inbreeding in the first four removes of his pedigree, Bahram carried no less than four lines of St Simon, who appears once in the fourth remove and three times in the fifth. While St Simon obviously contributes something to the merit of Bahram as a racehorse, his presence in Bahram's pedigree is remote. Most of the credit must go to Bahram's sire Blandford, to Concertina and to Friar Marcus, maternal grandsire of Bahram, a fast horse and also a successful sire. It is a true, well-balanced classic pedigree, embodying fine speed and adequate stamina.

Ribot, one of the greatest racehorses of the century, was bred by the late Federico Tesio, who unhappily did not live to see him race. He carried the colours of Tesio's partner, the Marchese Inchisa della Rochetta.

Ribot in make and shape was a perfect racing machine; technically he was impossible to fault, though like many Italian-bred horses he lacked the overall quality of the best examples of the Thoroughbred raised in England. In this respect Ribot did not compare favourably with another champion bred by Tesio, Nearco (Pharos-Nogara, by Havresac II), a horse of superb quality though not quite so well made behind the saddle as Ribot.

Basically, Ribot had an extremely tough, Anglo-Italian pedigree, in which classic, middle-distance sires, such as Pharos and Papyrus, were counterbalanced by stamina, through Ribot's sire Tenerani and the latter's grandam Try Try Again, and speed via El Greco, maternal grandsire of Ribot, and Bella Minna, dam of Tenerani's sire Bellini.

A notable feature of Ribot's pedigree is that it carries no duplication of a name in the first five removes.

Tenerani, sire of Ribot, was a tough, plain horse with ugly hocks, but a good racehorse, winning at all distances. A top-

RIBOT
b. 1952

				Rabelais
Tenerani, b. 1944	Bellini	Cavaliere d'Arpino	Havresac II	Rabelais
				Hors Concours
			Chuette	Cicero
				Chute
		Bella Minna	Bachelor's Double	Tredennis
				Lady Bawn
			Santa Minna	Santoi
				Minnow
	Tofanella	Apelle	Sardanapale	Prestige
				Gemma
			Angelina	St Frusquin
				Seraphine
		Try Try Again	Cylgad	Cyllene
				Gadfly
			Perseverence II	Persimmon
				Reminiscence
Romanella, b. 1924	El Greco	Pharos	Phalaris	Polymelus
				Bromus
			Scapa Flow	Chaucer
				Anchora
		Gay Gamp	Gay Crusader	Bayardo
				Gay Laura
			Parasol	Sunstar
				Cyclamen
	Barbara Burrini	Papyrus	Tracery	Rock Sand
				Topiary
			Miss Matty	Marcovil
				Simonath
		Bucolic	Buchan	Sunstar
				Hamoaze
			Volcanic	Corcyra
				La Soufriere

class winner in Italy, he won the Queen Elizabeth Stakes at Ascot and the Goodwood Cup. At stud Tenerani did not live up to his reputation as a racehorse and apart from Tissot (Premio Italia, Premio de Jockey Club), Derain (Italian St Leger) and the dual Ascot Gold Cup winner Fighting Charlie, Ribot was the only top-class horse sired by him.

It is interesting to note that successful sires sometimes emanate from stallions of no more than good handicap ability on the racecourse. Phalaris is one example, Marcovil (sire of Hurry On) another.

Romanella, dam of Ribot, was a good racemare; she ran only at two years and won all her starts, including the Criterium Nazionale in Milan. In all, Romanella bred six winners.

Ribot's tail-female line is a good, rather than an outstanding one. It emanates from Ribot's fourth dam, Volcanic, who carried the colours of the late Major Jack Courtauld to victory in the Lavant Stakes at Goodwood and bred for him four winners, including Cyclonic (Jockey Club Stakes, King Edward VII Stakes) and Typhonic (Park Hill Stakes), as well as Panic and Tornadic, both successful broodmares.

NIJINSKY
b. 1967

Northern Dancer, b. 1961	Nearctic	Nearco	Pharos	**PHALARIS**
				Scapa Flow
			Nogara	Havresac II
				Catnip
		Lady Angela	Hyperion	Gainsborough
				SELENE
			Sister Sarah	Abbot's Trace
				Sarita
	Natalma	Native Dancer	Polynesian	Unbreakable
				Black Polly
			Geisha	Discovery
				Miyako
		Almahmoud	Mahmoud	Blenheim
				Mah Mahal
			Arbitrator	Peace Chance
				Mother Goose
Flaming Page, b. 1959	Bull Page	Bull Lea	Bull Dog	Teddy
				Plucky Liege
			Rose Leaves	Ballot
				Colonial
		Our Page	Blue Larkspur	Black Servant
				Blossom Time
			Occult	Dis Donc
				Bonnie Witch
	Flaring Top	Menow	Pharamond	**PHALARIS**
				SELENE
			Alcibiades	Supremus
				Regal Roman
		Flaming Top	Omaha	Gallant Fox
				Flambino
			Firetop	Man o' War
				Summit

In assessing the breeding of a horse such as Ribot, consideration must be given to environment and outcrossing. Had Barbara Burrini, a useful racemare in Italy, whither she was exported as a foal, remained in England, the family might not have produced a Ribot.

Ribot's racing record is well known: sixteen wins from sixteen starts, including the King George VI and Queen Elizabeth Stakes, the Prix de l'Arc de Triomphe (twice) and an imposing tally of successes in Italy, embracing the Premio del Jockey Club.

At international level Ribot must be classed as one of the outstanding modern sires. Had he remained in Europe instead of being exported to the USA he might have done even better, as his stock as a whole were not suited to American racing conditions and training methods.

Nijinsky can be rated one of the best Derby winners since the Second World War and is probably the most notable son of the exceptional stallion Northern Dancer. Winner of eleven of his thirteen races, including the triple crown, and a top-class two-

year-old, his victories were gained with consummate ease. His
narrow defeat by Sassafras in the Prix de l'Arc de Triomphe was
the outcome for having too much ground to make up in the
straight and the probability that he was not at his best. The
reason for this was that he had an attack of ringworm before the
St Leger, and though he won that race he did not have a severe
task, achieving this victory despite traces of the debilitating
effect of the malady, which might still have been lurking about
him when he contested the Arc de Triomphe. In his final race,
the Champion Stakes, he had trained off, ran far below his best
and was beaten easily by Lorenzaccio. Nijinsky's downfall is
another instance of asking too much of a horse as a three-year-
old, instead of spacing out his programme over an extra season,
as in the case of Brigadier Gerard. Others to suffer the same fate
as Nijinsky include Shergar, Troy and Grundy.

A magnificent specimen, strong, powerful, well built, courageous and kind, Nijinsky is a fine advertisement for the Thoroughbred reared in North America (he was bred in Canada by E.
P. Taylor). Difficult to fault in conformation, he showed fine
speed as well as stamina, and that priceless quality, the ability
to quicken instantly. His career at stud has proved on a par with
his performance on the racecourse.

Brigadier Gerard is a tail-male descendant of Fairway, who
appears thrice in the pedigree of his sire, Queen's Hussar. His
dam, La Paiva, comes from the best branch of the Pretty Polly
family, is the dam of seven winners from eight runners and is
out of the dam of Stokes (Mieuxce), winner of the Windsor
Castle Stakes at Royal Ascot, the Spring Two-Year-Old Stakes
at Newmarket and second in the Two Thousand Guineas, and
several other winners. La Paiva, herself, was placed but did not
win, almost certainly due to her going blind in one eye.

Queen's Hussar, sire of Brigadier Gerard, was a good miler
about in the same class as Phalaris. He is inbred 3×3 to Fair
Trial, but bears far more resemblance to the latter's sire,
Fairway, than to Fair Trial himself. Queen's Hussar was a
beautifully made horse with a perfect set of limbs. He ran at
two, three and four years, winning seven races, including the
Lockinge Stakes and the Sussex Stakes. Before the appearance
of Brigadier Gerard, Queen's Hussar stood at a low fee and

BRIGADIER GERARD b. 1968

Queen's Hussar, b. 1960 — March Past	Petition	FAIR TRIAL	**FAIRWAY**	
			Lady Juror	
		Art Paper	Artist's Proof	
			Quire	
	Marcelette	William of Valence	Vatout	
			Queen Iseult	
		Permavon	Stratford	
			Curl Paper	
Jojo	Vilmorin	Gold Bridge	Swynford/Golden Boss	
			Flying Diadem	
		Queen of the Meadows	**FAIRWAY**	
			Queen of the Blues	
	Fairy Jane	FAIR TRIAL	**FAIRWAY**	
			Lady Juror	
		Light Tackle	Salmon-Trout	
			True Joy	
La Paiva, ch. 1956 — Prince Chevalier	Prince Rose	Rose Prince	Prince Palatine	
			Eglantine	
		Indolence	Gay Crusader	
			Barrier	
	Chevalerie	Abbot's Speed	Abbot's Trace	
			Mary Gaunt	
		Kassala	Cylgad	
			Farizade	
Brazen Molly	Horus	Papyrus	Tracery	
			Miss Matty	
		Lady Peregrine	White Eagle	
			Lisma	
	Molly Adare	Phalaris	Polymelus	
			Bromus	
		Molly Desmond	Desmond	
			Pretty Polly	

attracted few mares, but as a result of the Brigadier's success he was given a better chance by breeders, which he made use of by siring the One Thousand Guineas and French Oaks winner Highclere.

Brigadier Gerard's pedigree carries no inbreeding in the first five removes. It shows a blend of speed and stamina. Through Queen's Hussar, the latter's maternal grandsire, Vilmorin, and the family of Pretty Polly which, like the Picture Play family, has brilliant speed regardless of the stamina of the sire, speed is represented. Stamina is present through the Brigadier's maternal grandsire, Prince Chevalier, as well as Papyrus, paternal grandsire of Brazen Molly, grandam of the Brigadier.

It is a mile-and-a-quarter pedigree, and the fact that the Brigadier was able to win at a mile and a half in top international competition was due to his class, as opposed to intrinsic stamina. My personal opinion is that the Brigadier's best distance was a mile, since at this distance the state of the going proved immaterial, but beyond it heavy ground affected him adversely.

From eighteen starts the Brigadier won seventeen races,

including the Two Thousand Guineas, King George VI and
Queen Elizabeth Stakes, Eclipse Stakes, Champion Stakes
(twice) and Middle Park Stakes. Standing 16.2 hands, he had
perfect conformation, was tough, sound, courageous and possessed an excellent temperament.

These half-dozen outstanding racehorses represent no set pattern as regards pedigree. Of them, only Hyperion can be said to
have a 100 per cent blue-blooded pedigree; that is to say, he is
by a classic winner, who was a classic sire of consistent ability,
out of a top-class racemare from a classic tail-female line.

Bahram comes next by this measure, but his dam, Friar's
Daughter, was not so good a racemare as Selene, dam of
Hyperion.

Phalaris and Queen's Hussar, sires respectively of Fairway and
Brigadier Gerard, were not of classic ability on the racecourse.

Ribot's sire, Tenerani, was a failure at stud, apart from Ribot
himself, a couple of good Italian horses and the dual Ascot Gold
Cup winner Fighting Charlie.

Neither Ribot nor Fairway comes from a particularly distinguished tail-female line. Hyperion, Brigadier Gerard and
Bahram come from outstanding tail-female lines.

Hyperion and Fairway are inbred 3×4 to St Simon; the other
four are all the result of outcross matings.

If there is practical significance to be drawn from this data, it
is that breeding the best to the best does not necessarily produce
the best, and that a correct balance of the qualities most
desirable in a racehorse, not forgetting toughness, soundness,
temperament and luck, is the true secret of producing the best
racehorses.

This cannot be attained by following any set pattern, but is
the outcome of assessing correctly the characters which go to
make up the individual – conformation, racing ability, soundness, temperament, constitution, courage, speed, stamina – and
choosing a stallion or mare, as the case may be, best suited to
his or her opposite number. In other words, selection.

This one word, selection, embraces all the different patterns
of mating open to the breeder because, according to the individuals concerned, one mating may be best suited to an inbreeding,
another to outcrossing; one to the use of a highly-bred stallion,

another to the use of one of more plebeian parentage; one to the combination of two particular sires, another to a combination of two others.

It is a matter of careful study of all aspects, trial and error, flair and luck; and despite the greatest diligence, failure may result, since the genetic pattern to emerge is beyond control or prediction. At its gloomiest, the most a breeder can hope for is to reduce the margin of error; at its most optimistic, to strike on a mating which will result in a champion.

In either respect, the breeder's best guide is selection.

The more information available about the stallions and mares which a breeder intends to use when arranging his matings, the easier it is to arrive at the right selection. This information is widened when a stallion or a mare has been represented by runners, because then some guide as to the characters inherited by their progeny is available.

It is a great help when stallions tend to stamp their stock, both as regards conformation and performance; likewise a mare who tends to throw to the stallion is a valuable asset in helping to design a mating, since in both cases the outcome of a mating becomes less unpredictable.

St Simon, one of the greatest sires in Thoroughbred breeding, imbued his stock with much of his racing ability and appearance; all his foals bore a distinct resemblance to him and every one was a bay or brown, except the last foal he ever sired, which was grey. Son-in-Law and Wilwyn are other examples of sires who were pure dominants for bay or brown.

La Paiva, dam of Brigadier Gerard, invariably threw to the stallion with which she was mated, except when she went to the grey Donore (Fair Trial–Zobeida, by Dastur), the resulting foal, Delaunay, being a chestnut resembling La Paiva's maternal grandsire, Horus (Papyrus–Lady Peregrine, by White Eagle).

Until a mare has had two or or three foals and a stallion two or three crops to run, it is not always possible to discern, respectively, the type of mare and stallion likely to give the best results. Until then the breeding performance of each is not available and, as results show, a stallion's or mare's breeding performance can often throw up factors which were not predictable.

For example, La Paiva, though truly made and having clean,

sound, well-formed hocks, produced four foals with curbs. This may have emanated from a factor in the Pretty Polly family, since a number of its representatives, such as Sister Anne (Son-in-Law–Dutch Mary, by William the Third–Pretty Polly) and Colorado Kid (Colorado–Bay Polly, by Spearmint–Pretty Polly), two good racehorses from the family, had badly-shaped hocks; some of the less distinguished members were similarly afflicted.

This factor of curbs was one of the reasons why Queen's Hussar was selected as a mate for La Paiva, since Queen's Hussar had perfect hocks, sired stock with good hocks and, so far as I could see, had no sires or dams in the earlier removes of his pedigree who either possessed or transmitted bad hocks.

In my book *The Brigadier*, the reasons for the Queen's Hussar–La Paiva mating were discussed in detail. Briefly, they were the factor of curbs already mentioned; the fact that Queen's Hussar stood at a modest fee; that his conformation was excellent; that he gave me the impression of being a better racehorse than his form indicated; that he was tough, sound and courageous; and that he supplied the important factors of Fair Trial (twice) and Fairway (thrice), whom he resembled considerably, not present in La Paiva; and that the closest important sire in La Paiva's pedigree was Fairway's sire, Phalaris.

While a genetic pattern never repeats itself exactly in Thoroughbred breeding, this does not mean that a mating which a breeder has thought out carefully and believes to be sound is not worth repeating. The failures of own brothers to famous horses tend to receive much comment, and their successes to be overlooked. Often own brothers may be good racehorses, but differ in appearance and in the distances at which they excel. Blue Peter stayed well, his own brother Full Sail, a useful racehorse who became a successful sire in South America, was a ten-furlong horse; Dante, the best Derby winner of the Second World War years, had brilliant speed, while his brother Sayaji-rao, winner of the St Leger, was essentially a stayer; Persimmon, Diamond Jubilee and Florizel II were all good horses, the first-named pair winning five classics between them, but Persimmon was superior to Diamond Jubilee and the latter to Florizel II. Many other such instances can be found.

Thus, if a breeder sets his mind on a mating it is worth

repeating in case it misfires the first time. If it succeeds, he may prefer to try a different pattern.

The Queen's Hussar–La Paiva mating was repeated once more and resulted in a black/brown filly named Lady Dacre. She bore some resemblance to the Brigadier in conformation, but took more after her paternal grandsire, March Past.

Lady Dacre had ability and in the second of her only two races as a juvenile, the Devonshire Stakes at Doncaster, she finished second in a big field when sexually amiss, which affected her badly. She never raced as a three-year-old because she was perpetually suffering some mishap or other and at four, after running well at Newbury, trained right off and was retired to stud.

That consistency in own brothers sometimes occurs is evident in two other of La Paiva's offspring, both by Major Portion (Court Martial–Better Half, by Mieuxce). These were Town Major and Brigade Major. Both were winners and had ability. Brigade Major proved the better of the two, winning the Kempton Jubilee Handicap and two other races, but Town Major, who won at Sandown as a two-year-old, was handicapped by having jarred himself and frequently getting cast and injuring himself. Town Major resembed Major Portion, while Brigade Major had more of La Paiva about him. Both possessed excitable temperaments: Town Major would fly-jump his own height, Brigade Major kicked all the way up the canter; otherwise they were kind and intelligent.

The cause of their excitability was probably the combination of Mieuxce and Prince Chevalier, tail-male descendants of St Simon with a good deal of the latter's high degree of nervous energy about them, added to the highly-strung nature of the tail-female line.

I had been led astray by La Paiva's dam, Brazen Molly, having produced Stokes, a good horse, who was by Mieuxce. In combining Mieuxce and Prince Chevalier in the Major Portion–La Paiva mating, I overlooked the possibility of over-egging the pudding as regards nervous energy.

In the cases of Town Major and Brigade Major, their excitability and exuberance did not affect their racing performance, beyond making them training problems and liable to injure themselves. However, a further instance of paying insufficient attention to the aspect of temperament had a more unfortunate result.

This was the outcome of sending Bell Crofts (Arctic Time–Mrs Dale, by Impeccable) to Firestreak (Pardal–Hot Spell, by Umidwar) on the principle that line breeding to Pharos through his two best sons, Pharis and Nearco, had produced the Irish Oaks winner Ancasta (Ballymoss–Anyte II, by Pharis). In designing the Firestreak–Bell Crofts mating, I failed to take into consideration that, besides Firestreak's tendency to sire excitable stock, the mating produced an additional excitable element in Arctic Time's maternal grandsire, Colombo (Manna–Lady Nairne, by Chaucer), as well as a line of Mieuxce and a duplication of Hyperion. The outcome was an attractive grey filly named Lizzie Eustace – an ominous choice, readers of Trollope will appreciate. All went well to start with; she worked pleasingly, though inclined to be fidgety at exercise, and ran extremely promisingly first time out, finishing a commendable fourth in quite a good race after being slowly away. However, next time out, she got stage-fright before the race, did not want to do down to the post and petered out after running fast to half way. After being sold, she completely lost her form, but regained it to win several races; time and experience may have given her confidence.

To Queen's Hussar, Bell Crofts had bred a useful two-year-old in Eleanor Bold, and to Major Portion an even better one, Posy, who beat Be Tuneful as a two-year-old and also ran second to Rose Bowl in the Nell Gwyn Stakes and creditably in the One Thousand Guineas.

Temperament is a character which should never be overlooked; it is no use breeding a flying machine at home which disintegrates when it gets to the races.

Temperament goes hand in hand with nervous energy and faces the breeder with the problem of avoiding the former, at the same time introducing sufficient of the latter, which is essential to top racing performance.

In this respect, it is noticeable that highly-bred sires usually do best with unfashionably-bred mares. A typical example is Royal Charger (Nearco–Sun Princess, by Solario–Mumtaz Begum, by Blenheim–Mumtaz Mahal). A beautiful horse and a good one, Royal Charger was bought by the Irish National Stud, who reserved the right to select a number of the best mares available every year to send to him. Over the course of several seasons, these matings produced about two moderate winners. The best horses by Royal Charger were out of tough, unfashionably-bred mares, such as Sea Flower (Walvis Bay), dam of the Irish Two Thousand and St Leger winner, Sea Charger, and Bray Melody (Coup de Lyon), dam of Happy Laughter, winner of the One Thousand Guineas. When Royal Charger was exported to the USA, and mated with tough, outcross mares he proved an oustandingly successful sire.

Conversely, a stallion who has a tough, not particularly highly-bred pedigree tends to do best with highly-bred mares. An instance is Ribot, who was by the hardy racehorse and disappointing sire Tenerani and in whose pedigree the first important sire is Pharos, sire of his maternal grandsire, El Greco. Thus Ribot could be expected to do well either with mares carrying a prominent line of Pharos, the latter's full brother, Fairway, or those in whose pedigree a highly-bred sire such as Hyperion is close up. This indeed has proved the case, as is seen in the pedigrees of Molvedo, out of Maggiolina, by Nakamuro, by Cameronian, by Pharos; Romulus, out of Arietta, by Tudor Minstrel, by Owen Tudor (out of Mary Tudor, by Pharos), by Hyperion; Ragusa, out of Fantan II, by Ambiorix (out of Lavendula, by Pharos); Prince Royal II, out of Pange, by King's Bench, by Court Martial, by Fair Trial, by Fairway; Long Look out of Santorin, inbred 3 × 3 to Hyperion; and Graustark, out of a mare by Hyperion's son, Alibhai.

Going back to the theme of La Paiva, since it is of more practical value to take as an example a mare with which one is thoroughly familiar, having designed the mating with Queen's Hussar to breed a miler who might stay ten furlongs, we decided to try to breed a classic middle-distance horse. With this in view, La Paiva was sent to Royal Palace.

The principles on which this decision was based were:

Conformation. Royal Palace had a particularly good hind leg, as had his immediate antecedents. His chief fault was that he was a little back at his knee, whereas La Paiva has an exceptionally good foreleg. In all other aspects of conformation the mating appeared satisfactory.

Soundness. Though Royal Palace eventually broke down, due

to his being put out of his stride and moved off a true line through interference in his last race, he was in his third season of racing at top level. This was compensated for by La Paiva having particularly sound limbs and breeding sound stock.

Temperament. Royal Palace had a good temperament; La Paiva was inclined to be highly strung.

Courage. Both were courageous.

Racing ability. Royal Palace was an outstanding racehorse from six furlongs to one and a half miles, his pedigree indicating that he would stay further. La Paiva had a measure of racing ability and showed good speed. Her expectancy of stamina was ten to twelve furlongs.

Speed and Stamina. The mating suggested a balanced blend of both attributes, the speed coming from class (through Nearco, Phalaris and the tail-female lines emanating from Picture Play and Pretty Polly), as opposed to specialist sprinting influences.

Pedigree. The mating shows no inbreeding in the first five removes of the pedigree. Royal Palace is inbred $4 \times 5 \times 5$ to Gainsborough and $5 \times 5 \times 5$ to Phalaris. La Paiva is inbred 4×5 to Tracery and 5×5 to Persimmon and Cyllene.

Important factors present in the first five removes of Royal Palace's pedigree and absent in that of La Paiva are: Nearco, Picture Play, Pharos, Selene, Gainsborough, Sunstar, Solario, Donatello II, Havresac II, Bayardo, The Tetrarch, Swynford, Blandford, Teddy, Hyperion and Blenheim.

Important factors present in the first five removes of La Paiva's pedigree and absent in that of Royal Palace are: Prince Chevalier, Prince Rose, Papyrus, Tracery, Gay Crusader, Persimmon, St Simon and Pretty Polly.

This mating was carried out twice, the first resulting in an attractive filly, Cesarine (1973), the second in an imposing colt, St Petersburg (1974). Cesarine did not race as a two-year-old, owing to a major operation to remove a varicose condition on her girth. She raced once or twice at three years, showing a little ability, but may have been affected by her operation, was sold to France and bred winners. St Petersburg turned out well; second twice at two, he won at three and four years and was third in the Princess of Wales's Stakes. He was sold abroad. Both were good individuals, exactly the same colour as Royal Palace. Cesarine resembled Royal Palace behind the saddle, having La

CESARINE b. 1973 and ST PETERSBURG b. 1974

Royal Palace, b. 1964	Ballymoss, b. 1964	Mossborough	Nearco	Pharos / Nogara
			All Moonshine	Bobsleigh / Selene
		Indian Call	Singapore	Gainsborough / Tetrabbazia
			Flittemere	Buchan / Keysoe
	Crystal Palace	Solar Slipper	Windsor Slipper	Windsor Lad / Carpet Slipper
			Solar Flower	Solario / Serena
		Queen of Light	Borealis	Brumeux / Aurora
			Picture Play	Donatello II / Amuse
La Paiva, ch. 1956	Prince Chevalier	Prince Rose	Rose Prince	Prince Palatine / Eglantine
			Indolence	Gay Crusader / Barrier
		Chevalerie	Abbot's Speed	Abbot's Trace / Mary Gaunt
			Kassala	Cylgad / Farizade
	Brazen Molly	Horus	Papyrus	Tracery / Miss Matty
			Lady Peregrine	White Eagle / Lisma
		Molly Adare	Phalaris	Polymelus / Bromus
			Molly Desmond	Desmond / Pretty Polly

Paiva's forehand and forelegs and a head exactly like Brigadier Gerard, whose birth date she shared. St Petersburg had more of Royal Palace's head, neck, forehand and forelegs.

A factor of breeding which is sometimes overlooked is that, on the principle that breeding the best to the best does not always work out, when the optimum of refined breeding has been reached, it is necessary to breed 'down' in order to breed 'up'. In the days when breeders relied largely on their own stallions, breeding 'down' to breed 'up' was often done unconsciously, because there was usually at the stud a comparatively low-powered stallion, used on maiden mares, old mares and 'second eleven mares', who sired fillies which eventually became successful broodmares. The latter suited the highly-bred stallions at the stud. Typical examples are Chaucer and Stedfast at the Stanley Stud.

While far-seeing breeders are well aware of this and sometimes arrange matings thus, hoping for fillies which will eventually make broodmares, it is pure luck if a filly is produced. One breeder sent a mare four or five years running to Big Game for this sole purpose and got a colt every time!

The late Lt-Col. Giles Loder, whose stud was so ably managed first by Noble Johnson and on the latter's death by Peter Burrell, afterwards Director of the National Stud, as often as not sent mares to 'off-beat' stallions, fillies from these sometimes becoming successful broodmares. An instance coming to mind is Overmantle, by the handicapper Apron out of the brilliant Arabella. Overmantle bred Overture (Dastur), grandam of Supreme Court (Persian Gulf or Precipitation), winner of the King George VI and Queen Elizabeth Festival of Britain Stakes.

In the October 1969 issue of the *British Racehorse* I wrote an article on the problem of selection, embracing this aspect. The mare in question was La Paiva and the problem was to find a suitable stallion, standing at a modest price, likely to produce from this mating a tough, sound racehorse of reasonable ability which, if a filly, might make a broodmare.

The stallion chosen was Midsummer Night II (Djeddah–Night Sound, by Mahmoud), a top-class handicapper who won the Cambridgeshire and four other races.

The outcome was an attractive chestnut filly, Fille de Joie. When asked by a French friend how I could name a filly thus, I pointed out that her dam was a *poule de luxe*, which he admitted was apt. Possessed of brilliant speed, Fille de Joie won in good company as a two-year-old and, at three, the Hackwood Stakes at Newbury.

Theoretically, she should have stayed ten furlongs, but she barely got six. Possibly this was due partly to her having a leaky valve in her heart, a disability she outgrew by the time she retired from racing at the end of her three-year-old season, but she was so fast that it is doubtful whether, even without her trouble, she would have stayed a mile truly.

The problem then arose of choosing a stallion for her. Having purposely bred 'down' to produce her, it was essential to find a highly-bred stallion to restore the balance. At the same time, stamina had to be introduced to avoid breeding a pure sprinter, for which opportunities would be limited after the age of two, and classic hopes out.

The closest important sire in the pedigree of Fille de Joie is Prince Chevalier, a refined, courageous horse of top racing ability up to at least one and a half miles. Therefore it seemed a reasonable idea to inbreed to Prince Chevalier, provided a suitable stallion could be found, carrying Prince Chevalier close up in the pedigree. The obvious one seemed to be the Derby winner Charlottown, a son of Prince Chevalier. Moreover, Charlottown had a highly-refined pedigree, being out of that great racemare Meld (Alycidon–Daily Double, by Fair Trial–Doubleton, by Bahram–Double Life), winner of the One Thousand Guineas, Oaks, St Leger, etc. The resulting foal, Fille d'Amour (1975), was an attractive, well-made bay filly, with a sweet nature and delightful action. She had some ability, but probably suffered from being by Charlottown, who was a failure at stud. More successful was a handsome, smallish colt by Great Nephew, named Gros du Roi, who was placed in a nursery at Ascot and won in Scandinavia, including a Group I race.

The basic rules of genetics apply as much to breeding race-horses as to any other form of animal husbandry. These rules knock on the head such systems as those of Bruce Lowe and Vuillier, which are interesting studies but should not be followed in practice.

Also to be avoided are such often quoted terms as 'throw-backs' and 'bloodlines' in a literal sense, though the latter is a convenient term and harmless if no attempt is made to give it a literal scientific interpretation.

Perhaps the simplest and clearest way of explaining how genetic inheritance works is to take two bags, each containing an equal number of coloured marbles, including some plain glass ones signifying invisible recessive genes. Each marble represents a gene for a different character – coat colour, confor-mation and other hereditary factors, such as a tendency to break blood-vessels. One bag represents the genes contributed by the stallion, the other the genes contributed by the mare. Mix them up in one bag and draw out half the number of marbles. This represents the genetic make-up of the foal.

The more similar the genes supplied by the stallion are to those supplied by the mare, the more predictable the genetic pattern of the foal.

For reasons of finance, Thoroughbred breeding does not lend itself to intensive, planned inbreeding as with, say, mice, chick-ens or even cattle. Since only one individual (apart from twins) results from each mating, it is impossible to eliminate all undesirable factors at the same time as retaining racing ability;

1a. East Woodhay House Stud, near Newbury, Berkshire, where Brigadier Gerard was bred.

1b. Yearling colts at Plantation Stud, Exning, Newmarket. Horses like the choice of eating the heads of the grass or the shorter herbage, which this paddock gives them.

2a. Pretty Polly, ch. 1901, by Gallinule–Admiration,
by Saraband. Probably the greatest racemare
of the twentieth century and ancestress of innumerable
outstanding horses, including Brigadier Gerard.

2b. Sun Chariot, an exceptional racehorse
who proved a success at stud.

3a. La Paiva, by Prince Chevalier–Brazen Molly,
by Horus, dam of Brigadier Gerard.

3b. Lord Howard de Walden's mare Doubly Sure,
by Reliance II out of Soft Angels, at Plantation Stud,
Newmarket, with her 1980 foal by Sharpen Up, Diesis,
winner of the Middle Park Stakes and
Dewhurst Stakes and a successful sire.

4a. Tetratema, gr. 1917, by The Tetrarch–Scotch Gift, by Symington. A supreme example of the 'classic' sprinter.

4b. Gulf Stream, b. 1943, by Hyperion–Tide-Way, by Fairway. A rare instance of the combination of Hyperion on a Fairway mare, or vice-versa, producing a good racehorse. Winner of the Eclipse and second in the Derby, he had a light frame and a highly strung temperament. He became a highly successful sire in South America, being suited to tough, outcross mares reared in a different environment.

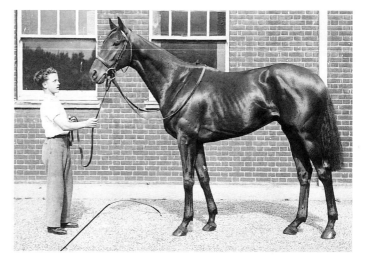

4c. Ribot, b. 1952, by Tenerani–Romanella, by El Greco. Unbeaten in sixteen races, he was one of the best horses in Europe since the Second World War. Technically perfect in conformation, he had brilliant powers of acceleration. He did not have the speed of Tudor Minstrel or Brigadier Gerard up to a mile, but had no flaw in his stamina. An outstanding sire who spent most of his career in the USA, he would probably have done better had he remained in Europe, since his stock were not ideally suited to American racing and training methods.

5a. Crepello, ch. 1954, by Donatello II–Crepuscule, by Mieuxce. But for unsoundness, which shadowed his racing career and made him difficult to train, Crepello might have proved another Ribot. Despite his staying pedigree, he had great speed and was a Derby winner well above average. Though a successful sire, a number of his stock had bad legs and were untrainable, which limited his scope as regards siring winners.

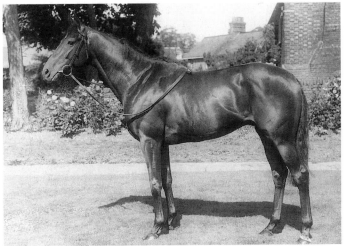

5b. Queen's Hussar, b. 1960, by March Past–Jojo, by Vilmorin. Tough, sound, courageous, truly made, with particularly good limbs, he resembled Fairway more than any other horse in his pedigree. Although not of classic ability on the racecourse himself, he proved a good sire and got the classic winners Brigadier Gerard and Highclere.

5c. Brigadier Gerard, b. 1968, by Queen's Hussar–La Paiva, by Prince Chevalier. With perfect conformation and an excellent temperament, tough, sound and courageous, he won seventeen of his eighteen races. With Tudor Minstrel, Timeform rate him the best English-bred horse since their ratings began.

6a. La Paiva with her colt foal by Royal Palace, St Petersburg, a winner twice and also third in the Princess of Wales's Stakes.

6b. Cesarine, La Paiva's filly foal by Royal Palace, a few days after her birth. She later bred several winners.

7a. Habitat (USA), b. 1966, by Sir Gaylord–Little Hut, by Occupy.
A top-class miler on ground which suited him (good or soft), his success
at stud was relatively greater than his prowess as a racehorse.

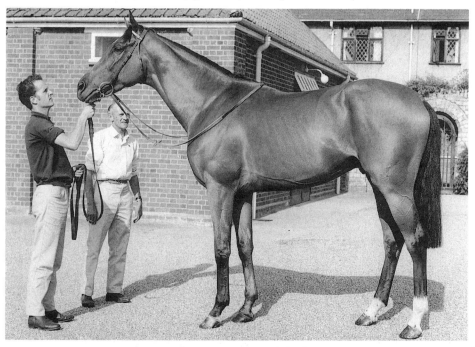

7b. Busted, b. 1963, by Crepello–Sans le Sou, by Vimy.
A top-class racehorse
and a consistent sire of good winners,
notably Mtoto and Bustino.

8a. Northern Dancer (USA), b. 1961, by Nearctic–Natalma,
by Native Dancer. A top-class racehorse, his pedigree is a blend
of the best American and European lines and he has proved
the outstanding sire of the post-war years.

8b. Sharpen Up, ch. 1969, by Atan–Rochetta, by Rockefella.
Unbeaten as a two-year-old, his best distance was probably
6 furlongs, but the stout blood in his dam's pedigree has enabled him
to sire a number of horses to stay considerably better than himself
and to win top races at middle distances.

9a. Nijinsky, b. 1967, by Northern Dancer–Flaming Page, by Bull Page.
One of the best post-war Derby winners, his thirteen victories
included the triple-crown. He combined speed with stamina and
his career at stud has matched his excellence on the racecourse.

9b. Mill Reef, b. 1968, by Never Bend–Milan Mill, by Princequillo.
The perfect middle-distance racehorse and one of the best in Europe
since the war, winning twelve of his fourteen starts.

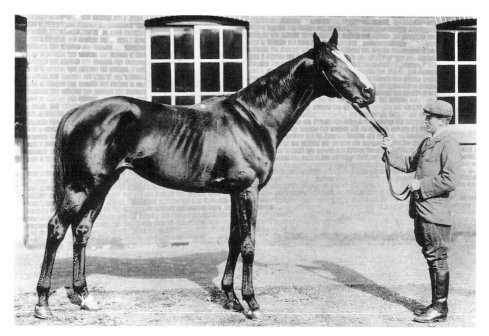

10a. Flying Fox, ch. 1896, by Orme–Vampire, by Galopin.
Inbred 3 × 3 to Galopin, this highly strung triple-crown winner
was exported to France, where he proved a great sire.

10b. Hethersett, b. 1959, by Hugh Lupus–Bride Elect, by Big Game.
Almost certainly unlucky not to have won the Derby, in which he was
brought down, Hethersett made amends by taking the St Leger. He is an
example of the union of a sire inbred to Tourbillon and a mare inbred to
Blandford. In a short stud career he sired the Derby winner Blakeney.

11a. Sea Bird II, ch. 1962, by Dan Cupid–Sicalade, by Sicambre. One of the best Derby winners of my time, he is rated by Timeform the leading horse in Europe since the war. A successful but not outstanding sire.

11b. Lynchris, b. 1957, by Sayajirao–Scollata, by Niccolo Dell'Arca. A top-class stayer who lived up to her pedigree. She is inbred 3 × 3 to Nogara, a classic winner in Italy and a great broodmare.

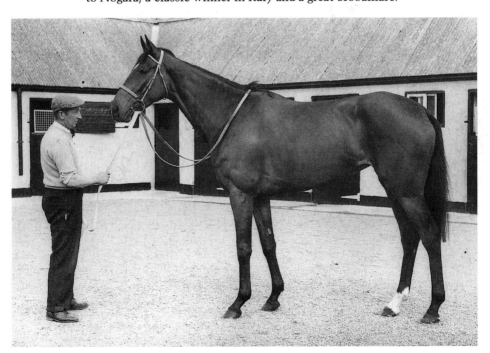

12a. Brigadier Gerard at stud, ridden by the author. Though it is not uncommon abroad for stallions to be ridden, this seldom happens in England. Insufficient exercise and boredom are detrimental to a stallion's health and happiness. If he gets too fat, his heart suffers, sometimes causing premature death; if he gets bored, his temperament may suffer. Since returning to regular exercise under saddle after three years' lapse, the Brigadier never looked better or showed more interest in life.

12b. The end product. Countess Walewski, by Brigadier Gerard–Gingerale, by Golden Horus, winning the Aldbourne Stakes at Newbury. Unbeaten in her only two races, she bred four winners.

and the object of the exercise is to produce a superior individual, not a breed whose members are all exactly the same.

While over a period of time, and by selection and inbreeding, a breeder might eventually produce a breed of horses which were fairly similar in all respects, it is unlikely that he would ever breed a champion, who is by nature something of a freak and, as such, would not conform to the general pattern, since nature abhors exceptions.

Thus the breeder must aim to avoid creating undesirable factors by injudicious matings and must realize that when he inbreeds he may be duplicating an undesirable recessive (not physically visible) factor, which will emerge in the individual. For instance, if a stallion and a mare each carry a recessive for bad knees, but possess good knees themselves, a mating of the two would possibly result in a foal with bad knees. This applies to outcross matings as well as inbred matings and, once more, points to the importance of selection.

An illustration of an incorrect interpretation of genetic inheritance, as expressed by 'merging bloodlines', is that it is *not* similar to taking a number of coloured inks, representing different 'bloodlines' from, respectively, the stallion and the mare, and mixing them together.

The 'marbles' example explains why the odds against a certain genetic pattern being repeated are great: each time the marbles are mixed and then divided, the odds against the same ones coming out are immense.

Another genetic rule is that when extremes are mated, the result is virtually never an exact mean between the two extremes; the offspring will incline towards one parent or the other. In practical terms, mating a small mare with a big stallion, or vice versa, will not necessarily produce a medium-sized horse; the individual produced is far more likely to be on the small side or the tall side. A better plan is to use a medium-sized stallion or mare, as the case may be.

This trend was illustrated when discussing the mating of pure sprinters with pure stayers as a means of breeding a mile-and-a-half horse. One of the few exceptions coming to mind is the Oaks winner Straitlace (Son-in-Law–Stolen Kiss, by Best Man), whose sire was an out-and-out stayer and whose dam won the Portland Handicap (five-and-a-half furlongs).

For some reason, which no one appears able to explain, fillies seem to produce more breeding surprises than colts. Apart from the example of Straitlace, it would be difficult to visualize a colt winning the Derby with the pedigree of either of the Oaks winners Lovely Rosa (Tolgus–Napoule, by Bachelor's Double) or Quashed (Obliterate–Verdict, by Shogun), whose sires were far removed from classic calibre, either on the racecourse or at stud.

Since the Second World War, racing and breeding has become more complicated than was the case before the war, owing to the international influence which has been introduced. Nowadays, as Sir Rhys Llewellyn emphasizes in *Breeding to Race*, the modern champion is more likely to have an international pedigree than one composed only of stallions and mares bred in the British Isles. In fact, so far as I can trace, the last champion to come into the latter category is Fairway. Nowadays it is virtually impossible to find a horse bred only from stock reared in any one country for, say, four or five generations.

In some ways this is a two-edged sword, since it is not so easy to find pedigrees offering a strong contrast, thereby providing material for producing hybrid vigour.

Astute breeders since the war realized that Germany provided a valuable source of mares and stallions which produced good results mated with stock bred in England or France. I use the term 'bred in England or France', as opposed to 'English-' or 'French-bred', since there is no such thing as a purely English, French, Italian, German, or US horse because pedigrees have become so mixed up.

The value of German horses (by which I mean those bred in Germany) is that for years the Germans have bred and inbred selectively from good, sound racehorses, evolving a distinct type. The chief sources were the descendants of Louvois (Isinglass–St Louvain, by Wolf's Crag), Dark Ronald (Bay Ronald–Darkie, by Thurio) and Festa, own sister to Desmond (St Simon–L'Abbesse de Jouarre, by Trappist). The late François Dupré was one of the first to use German blood, thereby breeding the brilliant Bella Paola (Ticino–Thea II, by Gundomar), whose grandam was French bred, being by Indus–Reine d'Ouilly, by Pharos. A more recent example is the 1975 Eclipse Stakes and Prix de l'Arc de Triomphe winner Star Appeal

(Appiani II), whose dam was by the outstanding German race-horse and sire Neckar; and the Derby winner Slip Anchor, by Shirley Heights, was out of a German-bred mare. His owner-breeder, Lord Howard de Walden, was the first modern breeder in England to appreciate German blood and has made good use of it.

An aspect of breeding to which breeders seldom pay attention is the ability to excel on hard or soft going; very few horses excel on both. The ability to go on hard or soft going depends, in the case of the former, on good feet, tough, sound legs and knees, a well-sloped shoulder and a daisy-cutting, as opposed to round, action.

Fluency in soft going depends above all, as Phil Bull explained to me, upon a horse's weight. A heavy horse sinks into soft ground, which results in his having to exert great effort to pull his feet out, whereas a light horse skims over the top. The size of a horse's feet are a minor factor, since horses with small feet often go well on soft ground, those with large feet often excelling on hard ground, and vice versa. A more important factor is action: a daisy-cutting action tends to make it more difficult for a horse to pull his feet out of heavy ground than in the case of one with a round action.

It is rare for a horse to excel on all kinds of going – Fairway was an exception – though a compromise can be achieved. An instance of a compromise is Brigadier Gerard, whose sire Queen's Hussar was at his best on hard going and whose dam La Paiva preferred it soft. Though able to win on any going, Brigadier Gerard was a much better horse on hard ground than in soft going and this was especially evident beyond a mile.

The Brigadier's versatility may have been due partly to his having a slight knee-action, which made it easier for him to pull his fore-feet out of the mud than if he had been a pure daisy-cutter.

The hereditary aspect of ability to gallop effectively on hard or soft ground is interesting and conforms to the principles of genetics. That is to say, mating a top-of-the-ground runner with a mud runner will not necessarily produce a horse equally at home on both, though it will help to avoid producing a horse totally incapable of galloping effectively on hard or soft going. Brigadier Gerard is one instance; another is Posy, by Major

Portion (soft ground) out of Bell Crofts (hard ground). Though not affected by hard ground as regards soundness, Posy could only produce her best form on good-to-soft going, having inherited this factor from her sire, to the almost total exclusion of the hard-ground factor present in her dam.

One aspect of selection, or rather lack of it, is to breed a horse with bad legs who can only produce his best form on hard ground!

7

Reading a Pedigree

A pedigree is of no practical value unless the breeder or student knows what the names in it might convey. This information is the only, if tenuous, guide towards the genetic make-up of the individual, but it is better than nothing and together with an intelligent assessment of the horse concerned may enable a fair guess as to his inherited characters to be made.

While recessive characters can sometimes be traced a long way back in the pedigree, these are usually undesirable rather than desirable; so that for practical purposes it is not much use looking beyond the first two removes for a direct source of racing merit. A study of the remoter removes is valuable in that it gives a clue to the type and source of the characters of the individuals comprising the first two removes, especially when inbreeding is involved, but if none of the horses in the first two removes has any merit as racers or producers, those further back can be disregarded, however meritorious they may be, because the desirable genes possessed by them have not been passed on.

In the accompanying pedigree (see pages 86–7) of Brigadier Gerard, it will be seen that all the horses in the first two removes had considerable merit as racers and/or producers.

Taking the case of his sire, Queen's Hussar: if he himself, March Past, Jojo, Petition, Marcelette, Vilmorin and Fairy Jane had all been useless racers and producers, the fact that Queen's Hussar is inbred to Fair Trial 3×3 and to Fairway 4×4×4 would mean nothing, since the genes providing racing merit possessed by them would not have been passed on.

However, as all possessed considerable merit as racers and/or producers, it is reasonable to suppose that some of the desirable genes emanating from Fair Trial and Fairway have reached Queen's Hussar, especially as he bears more resemblance to Fairway than to any other stallion or mare in his pedigree.

Brigadier Gerard himself was in appearance a balance between his sire, Queen's Hussar, and his dam, La Paiva.

In colour he took after Queen's Hussar, also in his hind leg. His head was something between that of Queen's Hussar and La Paiva. Since both Queen's Hussar and La Paiva were rather similar in type, it is not easy to hazard to which of them he owed some of his other characters, but in his exceptionally powerful shoulders and quarters there was a distinct suggestion of Queen's Hussar's maternal grandsire, Vilmorin, while in his hind leg the Brigadier resembled Queen's Hussar more than La Paiva.

From the notes on the horses comprising the first two removes of Brigadier Gerard's pedigree certain significant factors emerge. All were sound, truly made and courageous. The three elements of Queen's Hussar, March Past and Jojo represent speed rather than stamina, though both Queen's Hussar and March Past won at a mile. La Paiva, Prince Chevalier and Brazen Molly were all bred to stay a mile and a half, but only Prince Chevalier proved this at top level on the racecourse.

La Paiva's grandam, Molly Adare, was a sprinter and was by the miler Phalaris. The next dam, Molly Desmond, who won the Cheveley Park Stakes, did not stay either and was by Desmond (St Simon–L'Abbesse de Jouarre, by Trappist), a source of speed rather than stamina, though he sired that great stayer The White Knight, as well as Craganour and Aboyeur, who disputed the finish in the Derby the same year, Aboyeur getting the race on the disqualification of Craganour.

Brigadier Gerard's fifth dam, Pretty Polly, was brilliant at all distances, but the *forte* of her best offspring and immediate descendants has been speed.

Viewed as a whole, La Paiva's pedigree is one of stamina, with the strong factor for speed present in her second and third dams, Molly Adare and Molly Desmond. La Paiva's dam, Brazen Molly, is an unknown quantity as she never raced; her full brother, Bold Devil, was a useful horse up to ten furlongs, his best form being at a mile.

La Paiva was inbred 4×5 to Tracery and 5×5 to Persimmon and Cyllene, all powerful elements for stamina, this factor being closest up in her pedigree through Prince Chevalier, who came from an unbroken line of outstanding stayers, Prince Rose, Rose Prince, Prince Palatine, Persimmon and St Simon; and the Derby winner Papyrus (Tracery). One cross of Cyllene, that appearing through Polymelus and Phalaris, can probably be discounted as a source of stamina, since Polymelus was a ten-furlong horse and Phalaris a miler.

Thus, viewed as a whole, Brigadier Gerard's pedigree is a blend of racing merit at all distances from five furlongs to two and a half miles. Speed is more predominant in the early removes and this was one of the most marked characters of him as a racehorse. He proved able to win in the highest class up to a mile and a half and his best distance is a matter of debate; my personal opinion, as stated earlier, is that it was a mile.

Physically, Brigadier Gerard reflects the soundness, true conformation and courage so strongly represented in the first two removes of his pedigree.

By contrast, though having exactly the same pedigree as her full brother Brigadier Gerard, Lady Dacre's physical appearance invites a different interpretation, since she bore a considerable resemblance to March Past, being something between him and La Paiva. In training she proved highly strung, though having considerable racing ability as a two-year-old. Being accident-prone and not as constitutionally robust as the Brigadier, she did not train on, so it is not possible to make an accurate assessment of her racing ability or of her best distance. Though running up light in training, she was truly made, with clean, sound limbs, a good shoulder and not quite such a straight hind leg as her brother. When let down, she made a handsome broodmare.

Thus, as her appearance in training suggested, and on the evidence of her best form, Lady Dacre could be rated as typical of the better stock of March Past; and her resemblance to him supports the view that rational assessment of a pedigree can at times give some guide to genetic inheritance.

Bearing in mind that it is not possible to estimate the exact genetic contribution of any individual in a pedigree because there is no way of knowing the exact genetic composition of the product of the pedigree, at the same time it is useful to know the theoretical, mathematical contribution of members of the first six generations as expressed in Galton's Law of Ancestral Contribution. This calculation helps to put into rational perspective the contribution of any sire or mare in the first six removes of the pedigree, even though the proportion of the

BRIGADIER GERARD
b. 1968

by QUEEN'S HUSSAR b.
Good miler; tough, sound, courageous; truly made, particularly good limbs; ran up rather light in training; good but not too docile temperament; resembled Fairway more than any other horse in his pedigree; later proved good sire; got classic winners Brigadier Gerard, Highclere; at his best on firm going.

MARCH PAST br.
Tough, sound, genuine racehorse; 6–8 f. w.f.a. and top handicap class; well made, but lacking quality; prolific and versatile sire of winners of all types and distances; good temperament; raced for three seasons; not typical of any particular horse in his pedigree; stock mostly good handicappers, but he was not sent top-class mares.

JOJO gr.
Typical of her sire Vilmorin; strong, sprinting type; well made; good limbs and head; sound; won small 5 f. race at 3 years; first-class broodmare to all types of stallions; stock markedly superior to herself; distance of stock relative to that of sires; good temperament.

by PETITION b.
Top racer at 2, 3, 4 years; won Eclipse, New Stakes, etc. Successful sire; tall horse, well made; good temperament; sound and courageous; sired mostly milers.

by VILMORIN gr.
Top-class sprinter; won King's Stand Stakes; in build typical of sire Gold Bridge; strong, well-made sprinter-type; kind and courageous; good sire of fast horses; sound.

out of LA PAIVA ch.
Moderate racemare (possibly due to blindness in one eye); good speed stayed 10 f.; highly strung, superficially waspish but basically kind; truly made, sound, genuine, full of quality, ran up a little light in training; excellent broodmare, dam of 7 winners, all by cheap stallions; in type something between Prince Chevalier and Horus; good mother; inclined to get stock with curby hocks; best on good to soft going.

PRINCE CHEVALIER b.
Top-class racehorse, won French Derby, etc.; distance 7–14 f.; full of quality; well made; excellent limbs; little lacking in depth of body; sound, courageous; good temperament, but a little excitable, passed trait on to his stock; successful sire; effective on soft going.

by PRINCE ROSE b.
Outstanding racer in Belgium, also won Prix du Président de la République, France; won 16 races, 5–14 f.; fine individual; sound, tough, courageous; high-class sire, mostly of 1½ milers and stayers.

BRAZEN MOLLY b.
Unbroken owing to war; half sister to top-class stayers Fearless Fox, Challenge; dam bred other winners including a fairly useful full brother; grandam top-class 2-y-o and producer; kind, but highly strung; well made, rangy, good limbs, strong quarters, good head, but overall rather plain; rather down on pasterns behind; good producer, including Stokes (Mieuxce), 2nd in 2,000 Guineas.

by HORUS ch.
Well made, squarely built, tough, sound, genuine; fair racehorse, 5–14 f.; half brother to Flamingo (2,000 Guineas); moderate sire.

contribution is only theoretical and, indeed, might be considerably out.

Taking the figure 4,096 to represent the progeny, the ancestral
contribution according to Galton's Law is as follows:

2 parents' contribution is $\frac{1}{2}$ of 4,096=2,048=1,024 per ancestor in the 1st
  generation
4 grandparents' contribution is $\frac{1}{4}$ of 4,096=1,024=256 per ancestor in the
  2nd generation
8 g. grandparents' contribution is $\frac{1}{8}$ of 4,096=512=64 per ancestor in the
  3rd generation
16 g.g. grandparents' contribution is $\frac{1}{16}$ of 4,096=256=16 per ancestor in
  the 4th generation
32 g.g. grandparents' contribution is $\frac{1}{32}$ of 4,096=128=4 per ancestor in
  the 5th generation
64 g.g.g. grandparents' contribution is $\frac{1}{16}$ of 4,096=64=1 per ancestor in
  the 6th generation

Thus in the pedigree of Brigadier Gerard the ancestral contribution of his sire, Queen's Hussar, and his dam, La Paiva, according to Galton's Law, would be 1,024 each; that of Pretty Polly
(who appears once in the fifth generation) 4.

Fair Trial appears twice in the fourth remove, so his figure
reads 32 (twice 16); while the figure for Papyrus is 17 (one
appearance in the fourth generation, which gives a figure of 16,
plus one appearance in the sixth generation, giving a figure of
1).

While it cannot be stressed too emphatically that Galton's
Law must not be taken as an accurate assessment, otherwise
full brothers and full sisters would be exactly alike, it is a guide
within the realms of probability and, as such, helps to keep the
contribution ascribed to individuals in a pedigree within
rational bounds.

8

Important Names in the Modern Thoroughbred

Since the first edition of this book appeared, nothing has changed more than the important names in pedigrees.

As the years go by, names retreat further and further back in pedigrees so that soon they become purely academic. A concentration of powerful influences in the fourth remove deserves attention, but is unlikely to affect the individual to the extent of names closer up.

The most informative statistic upon which to base assessment seems to be 'Leading Sires in Order of Cumulative Money Won', taken from *The Statistical Record*, published by Weatherbys; and 'Leading Maternal Grandsires in Order of Money Won', taken from the same source.

The first list is given below, showing the leading six sires for the last six years.

Leading Six Sires of Winners 1985–1990
(in order of cumulative money won)

1985
Sharpen Up (Atan–Rochetta, by Rockefella)
Persian Bold (Bold Lad–Relkarunner, by Relko)
Welsh Pageant (Tudor Melody–Picture Light, by Court Martial)
Busted (Crepello–Sans le Sou, by Vimy)
Kris (Sharpen Up–Doubly Sure, by Reliance)
Green Dancer (Nijinsky–Green Valley, by Val de Loir)

1986
Habitat (Sir Gaylord–Little Hut, by Occupy)
Northern Dancer (Nearctic–Natalma, by Native Dancer)
Nijinsky (Northern Dancer–Flaming Page, by Bull Page)
Sharpen Up (Atan–Rochetta, by Rockefella)
Mill Reef (Never Bend–Milan Mill, by Princequillo)
Busted (Crepello–Sans le Sou, by Vimy)

1987
Mill Reef (Never Bend–Milan Mill, by Princequillo)
Habitat (Sir Gaylord–Little Hut, by Occupy)
Northern Dancer (Nearctic–Natalma, by Native Dancer)
Nijinsky (Northern Dancer–Flaming Page, by Bull Page)
Busted (Crepello–Sans le Sou, by Vimy)
Sharpen Up (Atan–Rochetta, by Rockefella)

1988
Mill Reef (Never Bend–Milan Mill, by Princequillo)
Habitat (Sir Gaylord–Little Hut, by Occupy)
Northern Dancer (Nearctic–Natalma, by Native Dancer)
Nijinsky (Northern Dancer–Flaming Page, by Bull Page)
Busted (Crepello–Sans le Sou, by Vimy)
Sharpen Up (Atan–Rochetta, by Rockefella)

1989
Habitat (Sir Gaylord–Little Hut, by Occupy)
Sadler's Wells (Northern Dancer–Fairy Bridge, by Bold Reason)
Caerleon (Nijinsky–Forseer, by Round Table)
Blushing Groom (Red God–Runaway Bride, by Wild Risk)
Ela-Mana-Mou (Pitcairn–Rose Bertin, by High Hat)
Nureyev (Northern Dancer–Special, by Forli)

1990
Habitat (Sir Gaylord–Little Hut, by Occupy)
Mill Reef (Never Bend–Milan Mill, by Princequillo)
Northern Dancer (Nearctic–Natalma, by Native Dancer)
Nijinsky (Northern Dancer–Flaming Page, by Bull Page)
Nureyev (Northern Dancer–Special, by Forli)
Busted (Crepello–Sans le Sou, by Vimy)

From this it will be seen that only six names appear more than
once: Habitat (5), Busted (5), Sharpen Up (4), Northern Dancer
(4), Nijinsky (4) and Mill Reef (4). To these might be added the
younger sires appearing in the 1989 and 1990 lists, Nureyev (2),
Sadler's Wells (1) and Caerleon (1), who seem likely to catch up
their elders before long.

Leading Six Sires of Dams of Winners 1985–1990

1985
Graustark (Ribot–Flower Bowl, by Alibhai)
Petingo (Petition–Alcazar, by Alycidon)
Habitat (Sir Gaylord–Little Hut, by Occupy)

Ratification (Court Martial–Solesa, by Solario)
Boldnesian (Bold Ruler–Alanesian, by Polynesian)
Birkhan (Alchemist–Cramouse, by Cappiello)

1986
Thatch (Forli–Thong, by Nantallah)
Drone (Sir Gaylord–Cap and Bells, by Tom Fool)
Match III (Tantieme–Relance III, by Relic)
Habitat (Sir Gaylord–Little Hut, by Occupy)
Hail to Reason (Turn-to–Nothirdchance, by Blue Swords)
Ribot (Tenerani–Romanella, by El Greco)

1987
Habitat (Sir Gaylord–Little Hut, by Occupy)
Hail to Reason (Turn-to–Nothirdchance, by Blue Swords)
Mr Prospector (Raise a Native–Gold Digger, by Nashua)
Northern Dancer (Nearctic–Natalma, by Native Dancer)
Petingo (Petition–Alcazar, by Alycidon)
Sir Ivor (Sir Gaylord–Attica, by Mr Trouble)

1988
Habitat (Sir Gaylord–Little Hut, by Occupy)
Blushing Groom (Red God–Runaway Bride, by Wild Risk)
Busted (Crepello–Sans le Sou, by Vimy)
Vaguely Noble (Vienna–Noble Lassie, by Nearco)
Crowned Prince (Raise a Native–Bay Hostess, by Royal Charger)
Bold Lad (IRE) (Bold Ruler–Barn Pride, by Democratic)

1989
Bustino (Busted–Ship Yard, by Doutelle)
Sharpen Up (Atan–Rochetta, by Rockefella)
Northern Dancer (Nearctic–Natalma, by Native Dancer)
High Top (Derring-Do–Camanae, by Vimy)
Habitat (Sir Gaylord–Little Hut, by Occupy)
Welsh Pageant (Tudor Melody–Picture Light, by Court Martial)

1990
High Top (Derring-Do–Camanae, by Court Martial)
Northfields (Northern Dancer–Little Hut, by Occupy)
Habitat (Sir Gaylord–Little Hut, by Occupy)
Artaius (Round Table–Stylish Pattern, by My Babu)
Roberto (Hail to Reason–Bramalea, by Nashua)
Nijinsky (Northern Dancer–Flaming Page, by Bull Page)

Turning to the list of sires of dams, it will be seen that those in the sires of winners list also in this one are: Habitat (6), Northern Dancer (2), Busted (1), Blushing Groom (1), Nijinsky (1), Welsh Pageant (1) and Sharpen Up (1).

HABITAT (USA) b. 1966

Sir Gaylord, b. 1959 — Turn-to	Royal Charger	Nearco	**PHAROS**
			Nogara
		Sun Princess	Solario
			Mumtaz Begum
	Source Sucree	Admiral Drake	Craigan Eran
			PLUCKY LIEGE
		Lavedula II	**PHAROS**
			Sweet Lavender
Sir Gaylord, b. 1959 — Somethingroyal	Princequillo	Prince Rose	Rose Prince
			Indolence
		Cosquilla	Papyrus
			Quick Thought
	Imperatrice	Caruso	Polymelus
			Sweet Music
		Cinquepace	Brown Bud
			Assignation
Little Hut, b. 1952 — Occupy	Bull Dog	Teddy	Ajax
			Rondeau
		PLUCKY LIEGE	Spearmint
			Concertina
	Miss Bunting	Bunting	Pennant
			Frillery
		Mirthful	North Star
			Dismiss
Little Hut, b. 1952 — Savage Beauty	Challenger	Swynford	John o' Gaunt
			Canterbury Pilgrim
		Sword Play	Great Sport
			Flash of Steel
	Khara	Kai-Sang	The Finn
			Kiluna
		Decree	Wrack
			Royal Message

Of those in the second list not found in the first, only Petingo (2) and High Top (2) appear more than once.

It is interesting to note that Mill Reef, though strongly represented in the list of sires of winners, is absent from the maternal grandsires list. So the leading six from the total of the two lists become: Habitat (11), Busted (6), Northern Dancer (6), Nijinsky (5), Sharpen Up (5) and Mill Reef (4).

While the influences of innumerable other names come into the modern Thoroughbred, the six mentioned appear most often. Therefore it is wise to give them close consideration, in order to try to discover in what way the best use can be made of them and what characters present in them should not be repeated by inbreeding, and if possible eliminated by suitable matings. (For Nijinsky, see pages 66–7.)

Habitat. A handsome, well-grown individual of good conformation, except for having rather small feet and knees and roundish joints. He showed his best form on good or soft going, winning the Lockinge Stakes, Wills Mile at Goodwood, the Prix de Quincey at Deauville and Prix de Longchamp and being second

BUSTED
b. 1963

Crepello, ch. 1954 — Donatello II — Blenheim	**BLANDFORD**	Swynford
		Blanche
	Malva	Charles O'Malley
		Wild Arum
Delleana	Clarissimus	Radium
		Quintessence
	Duccia di Buoninsegna	Bridge of Earn
		Dutch Mary
Crepuscule — Mieuxce	Massine	Consols
		Mauri
	L'Olivete	Opott
		Jonicole
Red Sunset	Solario	Gainsborough
		Sun Worship
	Dulce II	Asterus
		Dorina
Sans le Sou, b. 1957 — Vimy — Wild Risk	Rialto	Rabelais
		La Grelee
	Wild Violet	**BLANDFORD**
		Wood Violet
Mimi	Black Devil	Sir Gallahad III
		La Palma
	Mignon	Epinard
		Mammee
Martial Loan — Court Martial	Fair Trial	Fairway
		Lady Juror
	Instantaneous	Hurry On
		Picture
Loan	Portlaw	Beresford
		Portree
	Borrow	Tremola
		Booktalk

in the St James's Palace Stakes. He only ran at three years, and on ground which suited him proved a top-class miler. Habitat's success at stud was relatively greater than his prowess as a racehorse, his influence on the breed lying in his daughters rather than his sons, none of whom approached Habitat's merit at stud.

As will be seen from Habitat's pedigree, there is an inbreeding to Plucky Liege, 4×5, which is somewhat remote, and his paternal grandsire Turn-to is inbred 3×3 to Pharos. Thus Habitat was an easy horse to mate, especially with European mares.

Breeders using mares with Habitat close up in the pedigree would be well advised to aim at good forelegs and feet, especially if the mating shows an inbreeding to Habitat.

Busted. A tall horse – he stood 16.3 hands – Busted had a certain amount of daylight under him, nevertheless he was well made, good looking and combined strength with quality. Though his sire Crepello broke down, having suffered tendon trouble, Busted was sound and stood up to three seasons' racing. He did not run at two, but at three won the Gallinule Stakes and was

NORTHERN DANCER (USA) b. 1961

Nearctic, br. 1954	Nearco	Pharos	Phalaris	Polymelus
				Bromus
			Scapa Flow	**CHAUCER**
				Anchora
		Nogara	Havresac II	Rabelais
				Hors Concours
			Catnip	Spearmint
				Sibola
	Lady Angela	Hyperion	**GAINSBOROUGH**	Bayardo
				Rosedrop
			Selene	**CHAUCER**
				Serenissima
		Sister Sarah	Abbot's Trace	Tracery
				Abbot's Anne
			Sarita	Swynford
				Molly Desmond
Natalma, b. 1957	Native Dancer	Polynesian	Unbreakable	Sickle
				Blue Grass
			Black Polly	Polymelian
				Black Queen
		Geisha	Discovery	Display
				Ariadne
			Miyako	John P. Grier
				La Chica
	Almahmoud	Mahmoud	Blenheim	Blandford
				Malva
			Mah Mahal	**GAINSBOROUGH**
				Mumtaz Mahal
		Arbitrator	Peace Chance	Chance Shot
				Peace
			Mother Goose	Chicle
				Flying Witch

second in the Desmond Stakes and a lesser race, and once third. Sent from Ireland to be trained by Noel Murless at Newmarket as a four-year-old, Busted was not beaten in his four races, the Coronation Stakes at Sandown, the Eclipse Stakes, the King George VI and Queen Elizabeth Stakes and the Prix Henri Foy at Longchamp. These performances showed him to be a top-class racehorse.

Busted has proved a consistent sire of good winners, chiefly colts, probably the best being Mtoto, winner of the King George VI and Queen Elizabeth Stakes and Eclipse Stakes (twice) and Bustino, successful in the St Leger and Coronation Cup.

Busted is inbred 4 × 5 to Blandford and his pedigree is notable for having only one line of Phalaris – through the latter's son Fairway, followed by Fair Trial, Court Martial and Busted's grandam Martial Loan and his dam Sans le Sou. This made Busted easy to mate, in view of the many descendants of Phalaris in modern pedigrees.

Northern Dancer. A neat, compact, smallish but strong individual, Northern Dancer had plenty of quality, excellent conformation and a pleasant nature. At the time of writing several winners have appeared who are inbred to Northern Dancer, and he has proved the outstanding sire of the post Second World War years.

A top-class racehorse and winner of the Kentucky Derby, one and a quarter miles was probably his limit.

Northern Dancer has a true classic pedigree, his sire Nearctic being by Nearco out of a Hyperion mare coming from the same branch of the Pretty Polly family as Brigadier Gerard, while his dam is a daughter of the oustanding racehorse Native Dancer from a mare by the Derby winner Mahmoud.

Northern Dancer's pedigree is a blend of the best American and European lines, more or less equally balanced. The only inbreeding is the fairly remote 4×5 to Gainsborough, though his sire Nearctic is inbred to Chaucer 4×4. In tail-male both Nearctic and Northern Dancer's maternal grandsire, Native Dancer, trace to Phalaris, but too remotely to be of more than academic interest.

Sharpen Up. A well-made, neat individual of 16.1 hands, Sharpen Up was a top-class two-year-old, unbeaten in five races including the Middle Park Stakes. In his second season he failed to win in three attempts, but was narrowly beaten in the July Cup and finished second in the Greenham Stakes. Though excitable and a free sweater, Sharpen Up was courageous and of good constitution. His best distance was probably six furlongs, despite the stout blood in his dam's pedigree, which may have enabled him to sire a number of horses to stay considerably better than himself. Sharpen Up has a 3×5 inbreeding to Hyperion in the first five removes of his pedigree, which comprises a mixture of French, English and American stock, the top removes being American, the centre English and the bottom French.

Mill Reef (for pedigree see page 112). One of the best horses to race in Europe since the end of the Second World War, Mill Reef won five of his six starts at two years, including the Coventry Stakes, the Gimcrack Stakes and the Dewhurst Stakes. His single defeat was a narrow and perhaps unlucky one, in the Prix Robert Papin, by My Swallow, who was unbeaten at two and

SHARPEN UP ch. 1969				
Atan, ch. 1961	Native Dancer	Polynesian	Unbreakable	Sickle
				Blue Grass
			Black Polly	Polymelian
				Black Queen
		Geisha	Discovery	Display
				Ariadne
			Miyako	John P. Grier
				La Chica
	Mixed Marriage	Tudor Minstrel	Owen Tudor	HYPERION
				Mary Tudor
			Sansonnet	Sansovino
				Lady Juror
		Persian Maid	Tehran	Bois Roussel
				Staffaralla
			Aroma	Fairway
				Aloe
Rochetta, ch. 1961	Rocketfella	HYPERION	Gainsborough	Bayardo
				Rosedrop
			Selene	Chaucer
				Serenissima
		Rockfel	Felstead	Spion Kop
				Felkington
			Rockliffe	Santorb
				Sweet Rocket
	Chambiges	Majano	Deiri	Aethelstan
				Desra
			Madgi Moto	Ksar
				Groseille a Maquereau
		Chanterelle	Gris Perle	Brabant
				Mauve
			Shah Bibi	Pharos
				Hajibibi

top of both French and English Free Handicaps. In his second season, Mill Reef won the Greenham Stakes, the Derby, Eclipse Stakes, King George VI and Queen Elizabeth Stakes and Prix de l'Arc de Triomphe. His only other race was the Two Thousand Guineas, in which he was beaten three lengths by Brigadier Gerard, with his old rival My Swallow three-quarters of a length behind in third place. Mill Reef won his two starts at four, the Prix Ganay and the Coronation Cup, the latter by only a neck, due to his having a virus infection. He then fractured a leg and was taken out of training, luckily recovering to become a successful stallion.

A good looking, correctly formed, attractive horse of 15.3 hands, Mill Reef matured early and grew little, if at all, after two years. He had fine speed combined with stamina, being in every respect the perfect middle-distance racehorse.

Though Mill Reef was an outstanding racehorse with a superb pedigree, it would be unwise to inbreed to him. Like that great racehorse and sire Swynford, Mill Reef had brittle bones, and has passed this fault on to some of his progeny. However, he has proved able to sire top racehorses who stay twelve furlongs well.

He has an international pedigree with no inbreeding in the first five removes and was particularly suited to European mares.

Of the six sires exerting the greatest influence on the modern Thoroughbred in Great Britain, only Busted, Nijinsky and Mill Reef stayed one and a half miles. Habitat was a miler, Sharpen Up a sprinter and Northern Dancer's limit in distance was ten furlongs. Though Sharpen Up has stout influences in his dam's pedigree, and has sired a number of horses who stay fairly well, his influence on the whole is for speed.

Since the international championship distance is one and a half miles, breeders aiming to produce top-class horses at this distance must be careful to ensure that there is enough stamina in the matings to enable the progeny to get the distance. Proven stallions able to sire Group winners at one and a half miles, and without Northern Dancer, Mill Reef, Sharpen Up, Habitat or other important American-bred horses in the pedigree, will be needed for mares related to the above-named sires.

9

Inbreeding and Outcrossing

As mentioned earlier, inbreeding in Thoroughbreds is not possible in the same way as inbreeding with animals such as mice, when an intensive programme of close inbreeding over many generations can be carried out and a fixed, consistent pattern in a breed achieved. Inbreeding so far as Thoroughbreds are concerned is a pretty loose term, meaning little more than a name in one half of the pedigree being repeated in the other half. There are various ways of expressing these duplications, which for simplicity's sake are termed 'inbreeding', though in most cases they are too remote for this to be a scientifically correct expression. The clearest method would seem to be to express such repetition by a figure representing the generation or generations in which a name occurs in both halves of the pedigree. For instance, if Nasrullah were to appear once in the third remove, in the top half, and once in the second in the bottom, the individual would be said to be inbred to Nasrullah 3×2.

Similarly, 'line-breeding' is a term for which there appears to be no generally accepted definition. Most people regard it as a more remote type of inbreeding and it is probably simplest to stick to the same form of expression as used in the case of inbreeding, thus incorporating it in inbreeding.

While every Thoroughbred is inbred in some degree, however remote, for all practical purposes, if no duplication of a name occurs within the top and bottom of the fourth remove of the pedigree, this is considered to be an outcross mating. (Anything after the fourth remove is considered to be too remote to have practical significance.)

Breeders and students of pedigrees are apt to take it for granted that the genetic make-up of the individual is exactly reflected in the picture afforded by the pedigree. In other words, if a 3×2 inbreeding to Nasrullah is shown in the pedigree, the individual concerned must have a high proportion of Nasrullah's genetic make-up in his or her genetic make-up. In fact, since the choice of genetic pattern is so wide, even with inbreeding it is impossible to tell accurately what the genetic make-up of the individual resulting from that mating is going to be. One cannot do much more than make an intelligent guess as to whether a desirable genetic pattern may emerge or not. Beyond this the breeder has no control over the foal's genetic fate.

If a stallion or mare is repeated close-up in the pedigree, there is obviously a better chance of some of their genes appearing in the foal than if the individual only appears once, but it is no certainty. The situation is far from that in which mice who are own brothers and sisters are mated for twenty generations!

An instance of this was brought home to me when I arranged a mating between Never Say Die (Nasrullah) and Miss Print, by Grey Sovereign (Nasrullah). It was an abject failure, not because the less desirable characters in Nasrullah were intensified, but because neither these nor his desirable characters were evident in the individual at all. Instead, he was slow, phlegmatic, coarse and completely devoid of racing ability. To Sing Sing the mare later produced a useful racehorse.

Though a son of Nasrullah, Never Say Die was not at all typical of him and in all probability had little of Nasrullah in his genetic make-up.

Thus in designing a mating on any principle, whether inbreeding, outcrossing, line-breeding, or combining two particular, important, unrelated, successful names in a pedigree, which is known as a 'nick', the breeder must view the outcome with hope rather than confidence, because the outcome is so unpredictable.

Nevertheless, it is important to know the characters which certain important individuals possess and which may appear in their offspring, and to realize what might result, both on the good and the bad side, from duplicating such names.

It is no use merely looking at a pedigree and noting that, say, the sire is by Nasrullah and the maternal grandam is by Nasrullah, if one or the other, or both, do not by their appearance or behaviour suggest that much of Nasrullah is present in their genetic pattern. If this is the case, they are inbreeding to Nasrullah only on paper, not in fact.

Until some marked advance in genetic knowledge is made, it is difficult to see what more a breeder can do than by selection based on careful study, observation and deduction hope that he has achieved a mating which might produce a good horse.

Concerning inbreeding or any other form of mating, it is no use expecting to breed a good horse merely because the foal is inbred to an outstanding sire if the individuals through which such an inbreeding is made are no good. Flukes do occur, but to presume that they will do so regularly is equivalent to presuming to win a football pool regularly.

Having said all this, it might seem that there is no object in bothering about pedigrees at all and that matings should be designed purely on physical selection for necessary, desirable characters, such as racing performance, speed, temperament, soundness, etc. However, pedigrees are a clue to these characters and, related to the discernible character and possible recessives in the individuals concerned, give the breeder a better chance of knowing what he is about, if used intelligently, than if he ignores them completely.

The object of inbreeding is to endeavour to duplicate the desirable genes present in the stallion or mare to whom the inbreeding is made. Unfortunately, it is possible that the undesirable genes present may also be duplicated. In addition, it is not possible to predict to what extent the genetic pattern of the stallion and mare in the mating resembles the genetic pattern of the individual upon whom the inbreeding is based.

Allowing all this, inbreeding at least gives a chance of some of the desirable genes appearing in the foal. A much quoted example of successful inbreeding is Flying Fox, a brilliant racehorse and highly successful sire. From the pedigree shown here (page 102), it will be seen that Flying Fox was inbred 3 × 2 to Galopin, who himself is inbred to Voltaire 3 × 3. Further back in the fourth remove, Stockwell appears once in the pedigree of Orme and once in the pedigree of Vampire, who carries an additional presence of Vedette in the same remove. Much of this is largely, perhaps entirely, academic but the duplication of Galopin has significance.

To start with, Galopin was a good racehorse, winning the Derby; he was also an outstanding sire. Thus, while it can be argued that Flying Fox's racing ability came chiefly from his sire Orme, an extremely good racehorse and sire of the Derby winner Orby, since Vampire (dam of Flying Fox) was only of fair ability as a racehorse, Galopin's temperament was evident in Flying Fox, who, like Galopin, was highly excitable.

It is of interest that the Orme–Vampire mating produced six other horses. Of these, Flying Lemur (Ascot Derby) and Vamose (Prince of Wales's Stakes, Goodwood; Imperial Produce Stakes) were pretty good, Vane and Flying Leap won small races and the others were of no account.

This is a reasonable record, but does not really tell us a great deal; and it is worth noting that the vogue for inbreeding to Galopin 2 × 3, which followed the success of Flying Fox, had no conspicuous success.

Marcel Boussac, who experimented a great deal with inbreeding, produced an outstanding filly, Coronation V (see page 102), who was inbred 2 × 2 to Tourbillon. A beautiful individual with a nice nature, Coronation V won the Prix de l'Arc de Triomphe, French One Thousand Guineas, Queen Mary Stakes and other races, finishing second in the Oaks and Irish Oaks. She had one Achilles heel: she was a bad traveller. This could possibly be put down, at least partially, to her inbreeding to Tourbillon, since the latter had not the smoothest of tempers, which might have been reflected in Coronation V in the form of nerves.

Coronation V at stud never produced a foal, which was due to a veterinary disability unconnected with inbreeding.

The Eclipse Stakes winner Djeddah is another interesting example of inbreeding on the part of Marcel Boussac. Djeddah's grandam, Heldifann, was a full sister to Durban, dam of his paternal grandsire, Tourbillon. Djeddah was also inbred 3 × 4 to Teddy.

Inbreeding to mares is not so common as inbreeding to stallions, but there are a number of interesting and successful cases of this. A notable instance is Sansovino, a good Derby winner, whose sire Swynford was out of Canterbury Pilgrim, a daughter of Pilgrimage, dam of Sansovino's maternal grandsire, Loved One.

A more recent, successful inbreeding to a famous mare is evident in the outstanding staying racemare Lynchris, whose paternal and maternal grandsires, Nearco and Niccolo del'Arca, are both out of Nogara.

An aspect of inbreeding worth attention is that inbred mares, though they may be no good on the racecourse, sometimes turn

FLYING FOX b. 1896

Orme, b. 1889	Ormonde	Bend Or	Doncaster	**STOCKWELL**
				Marigold
			Rouge Rose	Thormanby
				Ellen Horne
		Lily Agnes	Macaroni	Sweetmeat
				Jacose
			Polly Agnes	The Cure
				Miss Agnes
	Angelica	**GALOPIN**	**VEDETTE**	Voltigeur
				Mrs Ridgway
			Flying Duchess	Flying Dutchman
				Merope
		St Angela	King Tom	Harkaway
				Pocahontas
			Adeline	Ion
				Little Fairy
Vampire, br. 1889	**GALOPIN**	Vedette	Voltigeur	**VOLTAIRE**
				Martha Lynn
			Mrs Ridgway	Birdcatcher
				Nan Darrell
		Flying Duchess	Flying Dutchman	Bay Middleton
				Barbelle
			Merope	**VOLTAIRE**
				Velocipede's Dam
	Irony	Rosebery	Speculum	**VEDETTE**
				Doralice
			Ladylike	Newminster
				Zulfika
		Sarcasm	Breadalbane	**STOCKWELL**
				Blink Bonny
			Jeu d'Esprit	Flatcatcher
				Extempore

CORONATION V b. 1946

Djebel, b. 1937	**TOURBILLON**	Ksar	Bruleur	Chouberski
				Basse Terre
			Kizil Kourgan	Omnium II
				Kasbah
		Durban	Durbar	Rabelais
				Armenia
			Banshee	Irish Lad
				Frizette
	Loika	Gay Crusader	Bayardo	Bay Ronald
				Galicia
			Gay Laura	Beppo
				Galeottia
		Coeur a Coeur	**TEDDY**	Ajax
				Rondeau
			Ballantrae	Ayrshire
				Abeyance
Esmerelda, b. 1939	**TOURBILLON**	Ksar	Bruleur	Chouberski
				Basse Terre
			Kizil Kourgan	Omnium II
				Kasbah
		Durban	Durbar	Rabelais
				Armenia
			Banshee	Irish Lad
				Frizette
	Sanaa	Asterus	**TEDDY**	Ajax
				Rondeau
			Astrella	Verdun
				St Astra
		Deasy	Alcantara II	Perth II
				Toison d'Or
			Diana Vernon	Hebron
				Gretna Green

DJEDDAH
ch. 1945

Djebel, b. 1937				
Tourbillon	Ksar	Bruleur	Chouberski	
			Basse Terre	
		Kizil Kourgan	Omnium II	
			Kasbah	
	Durban	**DURBAR II**	**RABELAIS**	
			Armenia	
		BANSHEE	Irish Lad	
			Frizette	
Loika	Gay Crusader	Bayardo	**BAY RONALD**	
			Galicia	
		Gay Laura	Beppo	
			Galeottia	
	Coeur a Coeur	**TEDDY**	Ajax	
			Rondeau	
		Ballantrae	Ayrshire	
			Abeyance	

Diezima, ch. 1933				
Asterus	**TEDDY**	Ajax	Flying Fox	
			Amie	
		Rondeau	**BAY RONALD**	
			Doremi	
	Astrella	Verdun	**RABELAIS**	
			Vellena	
		St Astra	Ladas	
			St Celestra	
Heldifann	**DURBAR II**	**RABELAIS**	St Simon	
			Satirical	
		Armenia	Meddler	
			Urania	
	BANSHEE	Irish Lad	Candlemas	
			Arrowgrass	
		Frizette	Hamburg	
			Ondulee	

SANSOVINO
b. 1921

Swynford, br. 1907				
John o' Gaunt	Isinglass	Isonomy	Sterling	
			Isola Bella	
		Deadlock	Wenlock	
			Malpractice	
	La Fleche	St Simon	Galopin	
			St Angela	
		Quiver	Toxophilite	
			D. of Y. Melbourne	
Canterbury Pilgrim	Tristan	Hermit	Newminster	
			Seclusion	
		Thrift	**STOCKWELL**	
			Braxey	
	PILGRIMAGE	The Earl or The Palmer	**BEADSMAN**	
			MADAME EGLENTINE	
		Lady Audley	Macaroni	
			Secret	

Gondolette, b. 1902				
Loved One	See Saw	Buccaneer	Wild Dayrell	
			D. of L. Red Rover	
		Margery Daw	Brocket	
			Protection	
	PILGRIMAGE	The Earl or The Palmer	**BEADSMAN**	
			MADAME EGLENTINE	
		Lady Audley	Macaroni	
			Secret	
Dongola	Doncaster	**STOCKWELL**	The Baron	
			Pocahontas	
		Marigold	Teddington	
			Sister to Singapore	
	Douranee	Rosicrucian	**BEADSMAN**	
			MADAME EGLENTINE	
		Fenella	Cambuscan	
			La Favorita	

out to be good broodmares. An example is Flagette, dam of
Herbager (Vandale), a high-class racehorse and a successful sire;
she is inbred 2 × 2 to Firdaussi, who himself is inbred 3 × 3 to
Chaucer. From the accompanying pedigree of Flagette it will be
seen that she is also, but remotely, inbred, 5 × 5 × 5 to
Polymelus and 5 × 5 to Flying Fox.

Another successful inbred broodmare is Miss France (inbred 2
× 3 to Asterus), dam of the Irish classic winners Talgo and
Fidalgo.

A pattern of mating which some breeders favour is to mate
unrelated parents who themselves are inbred, thereby providing
a sharply defined outcross with the aim of achieving hybrid
vigour. A case in point is Hethersett whose sire Hugh Lupus is
inbred 2 × 3 to Tourbillon and 3 × 4 × 5 to Bruleur, and whose
dam, Bride Elect, is inbred 3 × 4 to Blandford.

The inbreeding to St Simon evident in Hyperion's pedigree
has already received comment. A close look at Hyperion's
pedigree shows further repetition of names. St Simon's sire,
Galopin, is to be found through another source, Galicia, in the
fourth remove, while Selene (Hyperion's dam) is inbred 3 × 4 to
Pilgrimage.

Inbreeding in Thoroughbreds raised in Germany has already
been mentioned. A successful example is Orsini, a top-class
racehorse and leading sire in Germany. From his pedigree it will
be seen that Orsini is inbred 2 × 3 to Athanasius, also 4 × 4 × 5
to Laland and 4 × 5 to Dark Ronald and St Maclou.

Possibly the best use of inbreeding is in the case of a stallion
or a mare in whose pedigree there is a prominent, outstanding
individual surrounded by less distinguished names. An instance
is the One Thousand Guineas and Oaks winner Sweet Solera. In
the first three removes of her pedigree there is only one sire of
outstanding merit, Fairway. This offers an obvious invitation to
inbreed to Fairway when mating Sweet Solera. In fact, the best
progeny out of Sweet Solera was Bon Appetit, by Major Portion,
by Court Martial, by Fair Trial, by Fairway. This could be luck
and not the inbreeding, since the repetition occurs pretty far
back in Bon Appetit's pedigree. Nonetheless it is noteworthy.

Two successful racehorses and sires inbred to Fairway invite
comment – Queen's Hussar and Henry the Seventh.

The closest inbreeding in Queen's Hussar's pedigree is to

FLAGETTE
ch. 1951

Escamillo, ch. 1939				
FIRDAUSSI	Pharos	Phalaris	POLYMELUS	
			Bromus	
		Scapa Flow	CHAUCER	
			Anchora	
	Brownhylda	Stedfast	CHAUCER	
			Be Sure	
		Valkyrie	Eager	
			Flying Hack	
Estoril	Solario	Gainsborough	Bayardo	
			Rosedrop	
		Sun Worship	Sundridge	
			Doctrine	
	Appleby	Pommern	POLYMELUS	
			Merry Agnes	
		Birdswing	FLYING FOX	
			Game Chick	

Fidgette, ch. 1939				
FIRDAUSSI	Pharos	Phalaris	POLYMELUS	
			Bromus	
		Scapa Flow	CHAUCER	
			Anchora	
	Brownhylda	Stedfast	CHAUCER	
			Be Sure	
		Valkyrie	Eager	
			Flying Hack	
Boxeuse	Teddy	Ajax	FLYING FOX	
			Amie	
		Rondeau	Bay Ronald	
			Doremi	
	Spicebox	Spion Kop	Spearmint	
			Hammerkop	
		Sally Lunn	Swynford	
			Fireplace	

HETHERSETT
b. 1959

Hugh Lupus, b. 1952				
Djebel	TOURBILLON	Ksar	BRULEUR	
			Kizil Kourgan	
		Durban	Durbar II	
			Banshee	
	Loika	Gay Crusader	Bayardo	
			Gay Laura	
		Coeur a Coeur	Teddy	
			Ballantrae	
Sakountala	Goya II	TOURBILLON	Ksar	
			Durban	
		Zariba	Sardanapale	
			St Lucre	
	Samos	BRULEUR	Chouberski	
			Basse Terre	
		Samya	Nimbus	
			Sapience	

Bride Elect, b. 1952				
Big Game	Bahram	BLANDFORD	Swynford	
			Blanche	
		Friar's Daughter	Friar Marcus	
			Garron Lass	
	Myrobella	Tetratema	The Tetrarch	
			Scotch Gift	
		Dolabella	White Eagle	
			Gondolette	
Netherton Maid	Nearco	Pharos	Phalaris	
			Scapa Flow	
		Nogara	Havresac II	
			Catnip	
	Phase	Windsor Lad	BLANDFORD	
			Resplendent	
		Lost Soul	Solario	
			Orlass	

ORSINI
b. 1954

Ticino, b. 1939 — ATHANASIUS	Ferro	Landgraf	Louviers
			Ladora
		Freuenlob	Caius
			Farandole
	Athanasie	**LALAND**	Fels
			Ladyland
		Athene	Ariel
			Salamis
Ticino, b. 1939 — Terra	Aditi	**DARK RONALD**	Bay Ronald
			Darkie
		Aversion	Nuage
			Antwort
	Teufelsrose	Robert le Diable	Ayrshire
			Rose Bay
		Rosanna	**ST MACLOU**
			Rose of Jeddah
Oranien, b. 1949 — Nuvolari	Oleander	Prunus	**DARK RONALD**
			Pomegranate
		Orchidee II	Galtee More
			Orseis
	Nereide	Graf Isolani or **LALAND**	Fels
			Ladyland
		Nella da Gubbio	Grand Parade
			Nera di Bicci
Oranien, b. 1949 — Omladina	**ATHANASIUS**	Ferro	Landgraf
			Frauenlob
		Athanasie	**LALAND**
			Athene
	Oblate	**ST MACLOU**	St Simon
			Mimi
		Obilot	Cazabat
			Ortrud

Fairway's son Fair Trial, 3 × 3, but an additional appearance of Fairway is found in the pedigree, giving a 4 × 4 × 4 inbreeding to him. As remarked when writing of Queen's Hussar, there was far more of Fairway evident in Queen's Hussar than of any other sire in his pedigree, so it is reasonable to deduce that he had an appreciable representation of Fairway's genes in his own genetic make-up. If this supposition is correct, it would account for the number of horses by Queen's Hussar who stay better than might be expected, since Fairway, a St Leger winner, stayed well.

Henry the Seventh was by King of the Tudors (Tudor Minstrel–Glen Line, by Blue Peter, out of Vestal Girl, by Fairy Prince, by Fairway). Thus he was inbred 3 × 4 to Fairway, the closest important sire in his pedigree.

The outstanding, prolific impact of St Simon made it inevitable that inbreeding to this great sire would be practised widely, both by accident and design. Thus, besides Fairway and Hyperion we find many other notable winners inbred to St Simon, such as Adam's Apple, Aleppo, Apelle, Bettina, Colorado, Caerleon, Pharos, Fair Isle, Colombo, Watling Street and Garden Path, all of whom have a 3 × 4 duplication of St Simon, with in some cases, for instance Colombo, a further appearance of St Simon in the pedigree.

When a further concentration of an outstanding sire such as St Simon is produced, for example by mating Hyperion mares with Fairway, and vice versa, imbalance detrimental to racing performance may be the result. In this respect the combination of Hyperion and Fairway as sire and maternal grandsire in a pedigree, and vice versa, was a failure. Only one horse of classic standard came from this combination, Gulf Stream (Hyperion–Drift, by Fairway), winner of the Eclipse Stakes and second in the Derby. Gulf Stream was not an outstanding racehorse and in build was light framed, in temperament highly strung. At stud in South America, Gulf Stream did well, being suited to tough, outcross mares reared in a different environment. However, there are several instances of successful horses in whom there is a more distant Hyperion–Fairway cross, for instance the Yorkshire and Goodwood Cup winner, Apprentice (by Aureole, by Hyperion), out of a granddaughter of Fairway.

Inbreeding to an outstanding sire through his two best sons has sometimes given good results. An example is the Irish Two Thousand Guineas and Derby winner Museum.

Museum was by Phalaris or Legatee, the latter being his accepted sire and a pretty moderate one. Legatee in turn was by Gay Crusader, by Bayardo. The dam of Museum was Imagery, by Gainsborough, by Bayardo. Thus Museum was inbred 3 × 3 to Bayardo through his best sons, Gainsborough and Gay Crusader.

Another instance of this form of inbreeding is the Irish Guinness Oaks winner Ancasta, who represents a duplication of Pharos through his two best sons, Nearco and Pharis II. Ancasta was by Ballymoss, by Mossborough, by Nearco, by Pharos; the dam of Ancasta was Anyte II, by Pharis II, by Pharos. This gives a 4 × 3 inbreeding to Pharos through his two best sons, Nearco and Pharis II.

In the case of an inbred stallion or mare, the most suitable mating is likely to be one which produces an outcross.

Whether a breeder inbreeds or outcrosses should, I think, depend more upon whichever method appears to produce the best mating on the basis of selection, rather than upon the desire to aim at a particular pattern of mating on paper. In one

MUSEUM
b. 1932

Phalaris or Legatee, b. 1923	Gay Crusader	**BAYARDO**	Bay Ronald	**HAMPTON**
				Black Duchess
			Galicia	**GALOPIN**
				Isoletta
		Gay Laura	Beppo	Marco
				Pitti
			Galeottia	**GALOPIN**
				Agave
	Love-Oil	Amadis	Love Wisely	Wisdom
				Lovelorn
			Galeta	Ladas
				Galanthis
		Paraffine Lass	**ST FRUSQUIN**	St Simon
				Isabel
			Yvonne	Sheen
				Phosphine
Imagery, b. 1923	Gainsborough	**BAYARDO**	Bay Ronald	**HAMPTON**
				Black Duchess
			Galicia	**GALOPIN**
				Isoletta
		Rosedrop	**ST FRUSQUIN**	St Simon
				Isabel
			Rosaline	Trenton
				Rosalys
	Sun Worship	Sundridge	Amphion	Speculum or Rosebery
				Suicide
			Sierra	Springfield
				Sanda
		Doctrine	Ayrshire	**HAMPTON**
				Atalanta
			Axiom	Peter
				Electric Light

case a mating might throw up an inbreeding, in another an outcross.

Appreciating the danger of confusing cause and effect, as a matter of interest I analysed the pedigrees of what I rate as the eight best Derby winners of my time, namely, Hyperion (see page 61), Blue Peter, Windsor Lad, Bahram (see page 62), Crepello, Sea Bird II, Nijinsky (see page 66), and Mill Reef. (At the time of writing it is too early to rate Generous.) Of these, only Hyperion (inbred 3 × 4 to St Simon), Blue Peter (inbred 4 × 4 to St Simon) and Nijinsky (inbred 4 × 5 to Phalaris and Selene; his sire, Northern Dancer, being inbred 4 × 4 to Chaucer) show any inbreeding.

My feeling is that inbreeding can be of value, either directly to an exceptional sire, such as St Simon, or, indirectly, by mating an inbred sire with an outcross mare, or vice versa; or by mating an inbred sire with a mare inbred to a different source. But, on the whole, selection in the shape of a balanced pedigree, embodying racing class, toughness, speed, stamina, good temperament, correct conformation and soundness is the most reliable target at which to aim, and these qualities are

BLUE PETER
ch. 1936

Fairway, b. 1925	Phalaris	Polymelus	Cyllene	Bona Vista
				Arcadia
			Maid Marian	Hampton
				Quiver
		Bromus	Sainfoin	Springfield
				Sanda
			Cheery	ST SIMON
				Sunrise
	Scapa Flow	Chaucer	ST SIMON	Galopin
				St Angela
			Canterbury Pilgrim	Tristan
				Pilgrimage
		Anchora	Love Wisely	Wisdom
				Lovelorn
			Eryholme	Hazlehatch
				Ayrsmoss
Fancy Free, b. 1924	Stefan the Great	The Tetrarch	Roi Herode	Le Samaritain
				Roxelane
			Vahren	Bona Vista
				Castania
		Perfect Peach	Persimmon	ST SIMON
				Perdita II
			Fascination	Royal Hampton
				Charm
	Celiba	Bachelor's Double	Tredennis	Kendal
				St Marguerite
			Lady Bawn	Le Noir
				Milady
		Santa Maura	ST SIMON	Galopin
				St Angela
			Palmflower	The Palmer
				Jenny Diver

more likely to be found in an international, outcross pedigree than by inbreeding.

The term 'nick' has been mentioned earlier. Over the years, certain nicks have come to be regarded as a passport to breeding winners, for instance Hurry On on Bachelor's Double mares, Phalaris on Chaucer mares and later the combination of Nasrullah and Princequillo.

As in all breeding systems, nicks should be viewed with reserve and in relation to selection, rather than as a touchstone to success. Yet I do not think that the principle behind them – that a certain type of sire suits a certain type of mare – should be dismissed out of hand. The flaw in blind reliance on nicks is that all the progeny of a sire are not alike, having in their genetic make-up characteristics supplied by their dams, which can cause wide variation in horses by the same sire.

The aspect of nicks which makes practical sense is that certain sires tend to stamp their stock, a few to be prepotent for racing ability, these getting stock bearing more of their sire's characters than is the case with stallions who do not stamp their stock or are not prepotent. Thus it would be reasonable to

CREPELLO
ch. 1954

Donatello II, ch. 1934 / Crepuscule, ch. 1948				
Donatello II, ch. 1934	Blenheim	Blandford	Swynford	John o' Gaunt
				Canterbury Pilgrim
			Blanche	White Eagle
				Black Cherry
		Malva	Charles O'Malley	Desmond
				Goody Two-Shoes
			Wild Arum	Robert le Diable
				Marliacea
	Delleana	Clarissimus	Radium	Bend Or
				Taia
			Quintessence	St Frusquin
				Margarine
		Duccia di Buoninsegna	Bridge of Earn	Cyllene
				Santa Brigida
			Dutch Mary	William the Third
				Pretty Polly
Crepuscule, ch. 1948	Mieuxce	Massine	Consols	St Bris or Doricles
				Console
			Mauri	Ajax
				La Camargo
		L'Olivete	Opott	Maximum II
				Oussouri
			Jonicole	St Just
				Ste Fiole
	Red Sunset	Solario	Gainsborough	Bayardo
				Rosedrop
			Sun Worship	Sundridge
				Doctrine
		Dulce II	Asterus	Teddy
				Astrella
			Dorina	La Farina
				Dora Agnes

SEA BIRD II
ch. 1962

Dan Cupid, ch. 1956 / Sicalade, b. 1956				
Dan Cupid, ch. 1956	Native Dancer	Polynesian	Unbreakable	**SICKLE**
				Blue Grass
			Black Polly	Polymelian
				Black Queen
		Geisha	Discovery	Display
				Ariadne
			Miyako	John P. Grier
				La Chica
	Vixenette	**SICKLE**	Phalaris	Polymelus
				Bromus
			Selene	Chaucer
				Serenissima
		Lady Reynard	Gallant Fox	Sir Gallahad III
				Marguerite
			Nerva	Fair Play
				Zephyretta
Sicalade, b. 1956	Sicambre	Prince Bio	Prince Rose	Rose Prince
				Indolence
			Biologie	Bacteriophage
				Eponge
		Sif	Rialto	**RABELAIS**
				La Grelee
			Suavita	Alcantara II
				Shocking
	Marmelade	Maurepas	Aethelstan	Teddy
				Dedicace
			Broceliande	La Farina
				Reine Mab
		Couleur	Biribi	**RABELAIS**
				La Bidouze
			Colour Bar	Colorado
				Lady Disdain

say that quite a number of the stock of A are back at the knee and excitable and quite a number of the stock of B have good forelegs and are not excitable. Therefore, on the principle of selection, it is reasonable to mate A with mares by B, in the hope that the two will complement each other. If such a plan has a measure of success, it is at once hailed as a nick and is liable to be followed blindly; but there is no point in so doing if the mare by B is not typical of her sire, or if the nick is being brought about through a non-typical son of A and a non-typical daughter of B.

What makes more sense than following a nick purely on paper is, for example, if the breeder with an excitable mare who has bad forelegs says to himself: 'Where can I find a suitable sire who imparts good forelegs and temperament?' He may do just as well with a stallion who answers these qualifications and does not produce the nick at all; and he will certainly do better than with a mating which produces the nick on paper, but not the required characteristic in practice.

An aspect of mating worth noting is that outstanding race-horses who fall short of expectations as sires sometimes produce good horses through their daughters or from an inbreeding to such sires. An example is Gay Crusader, maternal grandsire of Djebel, and Clarion, the result of an inbreeding to Gay Crusader.

All this points once more to the conclusion that the most reliable guide to mating is selection; and that while pedigree can be a guide to selection it must be interpreted with care and the realization that it is only an indication of what *might* emerge in the genetic pattern of the foal, not what *will* be present in it.

MILL REEF b. 1968

Never Bend, b. 1960 / Milan Mill, b. 1962				
Nasrullah	Nearco	Pharos	Phalaris
			Scapa Flow
		Nogara	Havresac II
			Catnip
	Mumtaz Begum	Blenheim	Blandford
			Malva
		Mumtaz Mahal	The Tetrarch
			Lady Josephine
Lalun	Djeddah	Djebel	Tourbillon
			Loika
		Djezima	Asterus
			Heldifann
	Be Faithful	Bimelech	Black Toney
			La Troienne
		Blood Root	Blue Larkspur
			Knockaney Bridge
Princequillo	Prince Rose	Rose Prince	Prince Palatine
			Eglantine
		Indolence	Gay Crusader
			Barrier
	Cosquilla	Papyrus	Tracery
			Miss Matty
		Quick Thought	White Eagle
			Mindful
Virginia Water	Count Fleet	Reigh Count	Sunreigh
			Contessina
		Quickly	Haste
			Stephanie
	Red Ray	Hyperion	Gainsborough
			Selene
		Infra Red	Ethnarch
			Black Ray

Never Bend, b. 1960 (Nasrullah / Lalun); Milan Mill, b. 1962 (Princequillo / Virginia Water)

WINDSOR LAD b. 1931

Blandford, b. 1919 / Resplendent, b. 1923				
Swynford	John o' Gaunt	Isinglass	**ISONOMY**
			Deadlock
		La Fleche	**ST SIMON**
			Quiver
	Canterbury Pilgrim	Tristan	Hermit
			Thrift
		Pilgrimage	The Earl or The Palmer
			Lady Audley
Blanche	White Eagle	Gallinule	**ISONOMY**
			Moorhen
		Merry Gal	Galopin
			Mary Seaton
	Black Cherry	Bendigo	Ben Battle
			Hasty Girl
		Black Duchess	**GALLIARD**
			Black Corrie
By George	Lally	Amphon	Speculum or Rosebery
			Suicide
		Miss Hoyden	**GALLIARD**
			Miss Emma
	Queen's Holiday	Royal Hampton	Hampton
			Princess
		Cimiez	**ST SIMON**
			Antibes
Sunbridge	Bridge of Earn	Cyllene	Bona Vista
			Arcadia
		Santa Brigida	**ST SIMON**
			Bridget
	Sunshot	Carbine	Musket
			Mersey
		Stream of Gold	St Angelo
			Goldstream

Blandford, b. 1919 (Swynford / Blanche); Resplendent, b. 1923 (By George / Sunbridge)

10

Temperament and Soundness

Temperament has been touched upon already, but it so important that it merits further comment.

There are several guises in which temperament is to be found. It may be straightforward bad temper, evident in biting, kicking or generally savaging, or it may be lack of courage, refusing to fight out a finish or even to race at all. Further forms are nervousness, taking the shape of stage-fright, and over-excitability, resulting in the horse 'boiling over'. Added to these are extreme laziness and uncontrollable hard pulling.

Any undesirable temperament has a strong tendency to be hereditary and none is a help to racing performance. Thus it is important for a breeder to take careful note of the temperament of any stallion or mare from which he intends to breed, or which he contemplates buying. As in all facets of breeding, there is nearly always some drawback to any horse and the breeder must decide whether this is sufficiently counterbalanced by desirable qualities to justify its use for breeding.

Taking racing ability as the most desirable quality, this must be weighed against adverse forms of temperament. Probably the temperament least detrimental to racing performance is straightforward bad temper. This often goes with racing ability, while aggressiveness goes hand in hand with the will to win and, however uncomfortable for those whose task it is to groom, train or ride the horse in question, these trials may be repaid by races won. The most notable example is the great St Simon, who had a far from equable disposition which he passed on to a number of his offspring, notably the triple crown winner Diamond Jubilee, who was so difficult to manage that he could only be ridden by his stable lad, Herbert Jones. Rabelais was a pretty good racehorse in England and a most successful but bad-tempered sire in France. Rabelais's temper is to be found in several of his descendants, notably the Derby winner Watling Street. Tourbillon and his paternal grandsire, Bruleur, were also rather bad tempered; and many other good racehorses come in the same category to a lesser or greater degree.

The worst trait of temperament is lack of courage, since courage is one of the essential qualities of a top-class racehorse. To compensate for lack of courage, a horse must be of outstanding racing ability, so that he can win without being challenged or having to struggle. Conversely, a really brave horse will sometimes beat opponents of superior ability through sheer determination. On the whole, a courageous mare of moderate ability is a better proposition as a prospective broodmare than a brilliant jade. The former can be upgraded by a high-powered sire, while the latter may imbue a stud with a recessive yellow streak, liable to reappear at any time. The smaller the number of mares on a stud, the less risk can a breeder take in introducing lack of courage, since the possible necessity of culling and replacing the family may prove expensive.

Only the racecourse test will reveal the true nature of a horse's temperament. We had a filly who showed every indication of being genuine, having won in good style as a two-year-old and shown top-class form in her first two races at three. However, though never knocked about, she had a hard race on these two occasions, being flat out from start to finish; as a result, she never did her best afterwards, declining to take hold of her bit and only condescending to improve her position when the race was virtually over. This showed that she did not merit retention as a broodmare. Had she been retired as a two-year-old, or been raced only against poor opposition afterwards, her failing probably would never have come to light.

Fillies are more difficult to assess as regards temperament than colts, because of the nature of their sex. Three-year-old fillies sometimes do not train on, despite good juvenile form, simply because they become badly affected when in season.

Sometimes fillies are nervous or wayward, causing their form to be erratic, though basically they do not lack courage. The brilliant Sun Chariot (Hyperion–Clarence, by Diligence), winner of the One Thousand Guineas, Oaks and St Leger, was of the wayward variety. A problem at home, she only once declined to do her best on a racecourse, it is thought because she was not allowed to run her race as she wanted. There was a temperamental flaw in Sun Chariot's pedigree, her maternal grandsire,

Diligence (Hurry On), being out of Ecurie (Radium), a daughter of Cheshire Cat, who was notorious for her undesirable temperament and for passing on this trait. It is a difficult decision for a breeder whether he should shun a fault of temperament or try to breed it out. In a small stud, I am inclined to think it preferable to keep clear of mares carrying a factor for any form of lack of courage. Whether he is prepared to put up with bad temper or spitefulness is another matter; if he has to lead the bearers of this trait in and out himself, he may wish he had never introduced the factor into his stud, but if prepared to bite the bullet and put up with it, he may be rewarded with a Diamond Jubilee, Chaucer or Flying Fox. However, only if allied to the highest racing or producing performance is bad temper worth tolerating.

Nervousness, or stage-fright, is also a matter for consideration. Provided it is closely related to top racing ability and does not embody lack of courage, it can be tolerated, but the mares carrying it must be mated with great care to counteract the faults of their temperament. The immediate female descendants of Pretty Polly were prone to nervousness, yet correctly mated have produced some top-class, tough, courageous racehorses, like Colorado Kid (Colorado–Baby Polly, by Spearmint–Pretty Polly) and Spelthorne (Spearmint–Dutch Mary, by William the Third–Pretty Polly).

Extreme laziness may go with racing ability and courage – or complete disinclination to race at all. In the former case, it becomes a training and riding problem, rather than a breeding problem. Alycidon, the outstanding post-war stayer bred in England, is a case in point. Excessively lazy, both on the racecourse and at home, he raced in blinkers and would not exert himself on the training ground if asked to gallop further than five or six furlongs. Despite this, he was able to win the Ascot Gold Cup, Goodwood Cup and Doncaster Cup, the Jockey Club Stakes and King George VI Stakes and to run second in the St Leger.

Horses who pull unduly hard fall into two categories: those who are over-excitable and those who are determined to grind the opposition into dust from the moment they leave the start. The former are of little use for racing, since they are usually spent forces long before the winning-post is reached. The latter can be formidable racehorses. One such was the unbeaten Hurry On, who was never headed. Such types take more out of themselves than is necessary and thus are at a disadvantage with opponents who can be made to relax in the early stages of the race.

Temperament is a powerful factor in the make-up of a racehorse and is liable to be inherited. For this reason, it is advisable to consider this aspect carefully and, at all costs, avoid duplicating any form of undesirable temperament close up in a mating.

Equally important to temperament is soundness, and since good racehorses are often unsound, the breeder may find himself in a dilemma when it comes to choosing a stallion to use.

This particularly affects an owner-breeder with a small stud, who could find himself with nothing to race, whereas a breeder with many mares has resources on which to fall back.

The breeder can choose either to take a risk with a stallion who has a hereditary unsoundness but great racing ability, hoping to counteract the failing by sending him a sound mare, or to play for safety by shunning him altogether.

That great German breeder of the past, Count Lehndorff, put soundness above all qualities, and there is much to support his view. As a breeder with only two mares, I agree with him, as it is usually possible to find a suitable alternative stallion, and it is no use having a brilliant racehorse who will not stand up to racing and a mare who breeds similar stock. With a large number of mares to be mated, a breeder may have to take the risk, but if the outcome is unsound, he will be well advised to cull it from his stud.

On no account should inbreeding take place with unsound stock. François de Brignac, racing manager to Marcel Boussac, once told me that they had several horses inbred to Blandford, all of whom broke down.

Though Blandford himself was sound – he had an accident in the paddock as a yearling, which led to some people accusing him wrongly of hereditary unsoundness – his sire Swynford broke down and a number of his descendants inherited his weakness to brittle bones, resulting in split pasterns and similar injuries.

A breeder may have the misfortune to acquire a perfectly

sound mare, only to find that she has a recessive factor for unsoundness, which she passes on to her offspring. The only solution is to get rid of her or not breed from her.

Unfortunately, too many top racehorses are retired before they have been properly tested on the racecourse, so that it is not possible to discover how tough and sound they are. Conversely, some really tough, sound sires – Ardross is a typical example – are neglected because they have an unfashionable pedigree and have been exploited in staying races.

Maintaining Continuity

In breeding racehorses the situation changes with each successive generation. To devise a set pattern of mating and stick to it is to invite eventual disaster. This principle is evident in the gradual loss of speed experienced by breeders with classic ambitions, who have planned virtually every mating to produce a top horse at a mile and a half, the distance of the Derby and the accepted one for Group I champion races.

While a top-class mile-and-a-half racehorse must have really good speed, it is necessary for him to have stamina in his pedigree as well; but continued mating of horses excelling at a mile and a half, or further, is liable to result in loss of speed. Since speed is the basic quality of the racehorse, this is fatal. The continued mating of mile-and-a-half horses may result in success in winners of 'cup' races and important long-distance handicaps, but it is not so likely to produce the top mile-and-a-half runner, let alone a good horse at ten furlongs or a mile. The loss of speed may be gradual in a stud breeding exclusively for a mile and a half or further, but once it has taken place, a point of no return may be reached, since it is extremely difficult to graft speed onto a family that has lost it, even by the aid of fast stallions. At best, a fast plodder is likely to result, and since the ability to quicken is one of the most valuable assets of a racehorse, the last case is only a little better than the first.

Such a fate overtook the Cliveden Stud, which after the Second World War had consistent success at classic level, hardly a year going by without an Astor horse being placed in a classic if not winning one. Later, however, its best winners tended to be pure stayers.

The late Aga Khan never fell into the trap of losing speed in his stud. Though making use of staying sires, he regularly mated a proportion of his mares for pure speed.

As noted earlier, there is a distinction between the professional sprinter, such as Gold Bridge, a number of his sons, for instance Vilmorin, and stallions of a similar category, such as

Sir Cosmo and his son Panorama, and the classic sprinter represented by Tetratema, Tudor Minstrel, Abernant, My Babu and, more recently, Habitat.

Introduction of speed through the specialist sprinter, whose limit is six furlongs, usually means that it is necessary to have a fallow generation – perhaps even two – before a true mile-and-a-half classic horse is produced, whereas by the introduction of the classic sprinter, most commonly represented by a Two Thousand Guineas horse or a horse with a middle-distance pedigree who was a sprinter, e.g. Friar Marcus, the breeder is more likely to do it in one.

At the same time, a breeder must be realistic and have racing ability uppermost in his mind; he cannot win classic races the whole time and a good mare by a professional sprinter is more likely to breed him a decent winner than is a bad one by a classic sprinter. Besides, the former might enable him to achieve a classic objective later on. For instance, the grandam of Park Top (Kalydon–Nellie Park, by Arctic Prince), a brilliant mare at a mile and a half in championship class, was by the professional sprinter Denturius (Gold Bridge).

Thus it is prudent for a breeder, even if the twelve-furlong champion is his chief aim, frequently to use stallions who get fast horses. In this respect it is not a bad plan to make a point of sending maiden mares to a fast horse, to start them off, hoping to get a filly likely to make a broodmare.

In defence of the policy of classic breeders operating between the two wars, it must be appreciated that in those days the Ascot Gold Cup (two and a half miles) held a status equivalent to that of the King George VI and Queen Elizabeth Stakes today, so breeders at top level always had this in mind, designing their matings to produce a horse to win the Derby and go on to take the Ascot Gold Cup the following year. Nowadays, provided a horse can prove a champion up to a mile and a half, no one worries about his ability beyond this distance. Thus speed in the middle-distance classic sphere has become an even more powerful factor than it was before 1939.

Since no situation in racehorse breeding is static, breeders will soon find themselves having to use sires with stamina beyond one and a half miles in order to keep ahead of the game, as over-concentration on speed will gradually result in short runners; and the breeder who can produce a horse able to stay better than his rivals and possessing comparable speed will have the edge on the others. Therefore to maintain continuity at top level in his stud a breeder must establish a nice balance between speed and stamina, keeping a close watch on the situation, so that he does not find his stud moving to either of the extremes of short runners or plodders.

Another danger of studs operating at classic level is for the stock to become over-bred, deteriorating as a result. In this respect a breeder must be prepared to waste a generation by sending a too highly-bred mare to a stallion who is not too highly bred, to re-establish the balance. The main objective of this type of mating is to get a filly likely to make a broodmare; but even if he breeds a colt it is probable that the latter will turn out to be a better racehorse than one by a highly-bred sire. The resulting foal is unlikely to prove up to classic-winning standard, but a good racehorse below classic-winning standard, however he is bred, is better than a bad one with a classic pedigree. Moreover, examination of the breeding of the first three horses in the Derby as often as not reveals one with a distinctly plebeian pedigree.

An interesting example of the maintenance of speed in a stud with the production of a classic stayer resulting is to be seen in the tail-female line of the St Leger winner Premonition (Precipitation), who also finished first in the Irish Derby, though losing the race on a disqualification.

Premonition's third dam is Golden Silence (Swynford–Molly Desmond, by Desmond–Pretty Polly), a high-class racemare who finished third in the Oaks. Mated with the classic sprinter Tetratema (The Tetrarch–Scotch Gift, by Symington), Golden Silence produced Tip the Wink, a good two-year-old who did not train on. Tip the Wink in turn was mated with Fair Trial (Fairway–Lady Juror, by Son-in-Law), who despite his pedigree was only a miler, though a really good one. The outcome was a filly called Trial Ground, who won a small race as a two-year-old but had a nice turn of speed. Hitherto all the mares mentioned – Golden Silence, Tip the Wink and Trial Ground – were bred at the late Lt-Col. Giles Loder's Eyrefield Stud in Ireland and carried his 'yellow, dark blue sleeves, black cap'. One of the principles of this stud was never to lose speed, and while frequent use was made of middle-distance and staying sires, most of the mares went to a fast horse at some time in their stud life.

At the end of her racing career, Trial Ground was bought by the Dunchurch Lodge Stud and sent to Precipitation, the outcome being Premonition.

In the case of the La Paiva family in our own stud, there were three fillies out of the mare: Fille de Joie (Midsummer Night II), Lady Dacre (Queen's Hussar) and Cesarine (Royal Palace).

At the moment (1991) there is only one brood mare tracing to La Paiva, namely Princess Lieven (by Royal Palace–Lady Dacre). Unraced, because she did not stay more than three furlongs, but flew for the distance, she is dam of a winner, Beau Ideal (by Brigadier Gerard), who represents a brother–sister inbreeding.

We hope the family will be continued through Anonymous (Night Shift–Princess Lieven), foaled in 1990, on looks and action the best filly we have bred. However, only performance on the racecourse and at stud counts.

To maintain a stud at top level, a breeder must plan as if he is going to live for ever. A 'things will see me out' attitude is certain to result in deterioration, and for all he knows he may run on into a vigorous old age, as did Federico Tesio and the late Lord Rosebery. In this case, if he has let things slide, using indifferent sires because they are cheap, and inexpensive professional sprinters, his declining years will be clouded by seeing his colours carried by moderate handicappers. Though he did not live to see him race, Tesio bred Ribot at the end of his life, leaving a great inheritance to posterity.

One fallacy common among breeders is to hang on to mares going back to a foundation mare of merit, even though these descendants have deteriorated greatly from the original source, which is now three or four generations away. A breeder has a natural, sentimental attachment to descendants of a favourite mare, but to avoid the stud going downhill sentiment must not be allowed to displace realism. Every mare should be assessed as an individual, regardless of her tap-root, and viewed in the same light as that in which the breeder would regard her were he considering buying her for his stud. Thus it is prudent to tolerate only one dud representative, as regards racing and/or producing merit, after the original source and, in terms of 'families' mentally to replace the tap-root by the next good producer. For instance, the immediate descendants of Pretty Polly's daughter Molly Desmond become the Molly Desmond family; those of Molly Adare the Molly Adare family and so on to La Paiva. Though La Paiva is a descendant of Pretty Polly, and therefore belongs to the Pretty Polly family, it is more realistic to regard her as a member of the family of her dam, Brazen Molly. Once a breeder has developed this way of thinking, he will not fall into the trap of hanging on to bad daughters of bad mares, merely because they trace to a favourite tap-root. It is far wiser to put sentiment aside, get rid of such a mare and replace her with another, chosen on the principles set out earlier.

A more difficult problem is the gradual deterioration of the descendants of a good tap-root; they continue to win, but in races of lessening importance.

When this occurs with ominous consistency, despite the use of good stallions chosen on a rational principle of selection, something is wrong. If the representatives of other families on the stud continue to prosper and as a whole do as well as or better than their breeding suggests, the indication is that there is nothing amiss with the environment or management of the stud. The deduction therefore must be that the aforesaid family is running down. Since it is no use breeding from mares whose stock are not so good as they should be, it is as well to harden one's heart and get out of the family before the bubble bursts and buyers awaken to its deterioration. This deterioration may possibly be due to successive mares having been bred and reared on the same land, generation after generation, and the need for a different environment. Thus if such mares are sold and prove highly successful for someone else, it is no use bemoaning the fact; the chances are that neither they nor their descendants would have achieved comparable success had they been retained. One way round this particular problem is for a breeder to board out a mare whose tail-female antecedents have been on the same land for several generations, or exchange her with another breeder for a mare whose family have been on his stud for several generations. On this principle Sir John Astor bred the Irish Two Thousand Guineas winner Sharp Edge (Silver Shark–Cutle, by Saint Crespin III), whose grandam Cutter (Donatello

II–Felucca, by Nearco) was bred and raced by Dick Hollingsworth.

Owing to the uncertainty of breeding racehorses, a breeder is sure, sooner or later, to sell what turns out to be the wrong mare. He must face the prospect with equanimity, however, for sell he must unless his stud becomes overstocked or he is prepared to keep expanding.

Everyone has his own philosophy and methods in breeding racehorses, and it is not a bad plan for a breeder to have in mind a blueprint of the general type of stock he wishes to produce. Most breeders have only one idea: to produce winners, regardless of what they look like. This, after all, is the object of the exercise and in a large stud is a more or less inevitable policy. A small stud, on the other hand, can be more selective in the matter of choice. My own aim, apart from trying to breed winners, is to produce sound, truly made, courageous, good-tempered individuals, combining quality with substance, neither outsized nor undersized – all of more or less the same stamp. On the whole I prefer mares under 16 hands. With only a couple of mares, a wide range of stallions is available, so that it is possible to mate selectively for a particular type. Studs which hold to a principle of keeping a certain type in mind gradually develop a breed distinctive of it. This has advantages in that buyers of the surplus stock know what they are likely to get, and the task of mating is made easier both for them and the breeder himself if selection for desirable factors and a good type of individual has been maintained through successive generations.

A problem arises when a breeder produces a good filly, who proves to have a serious flaw, such as unsoundness of wind or limb, breaks blood-vessels, has a bad temper or lacks courage. Does he get rid of her, on the principle that he would not buy her as a prospective broodmare, or does he try to correct the flaw by selective mating, hoping at the same time to preserve her brilliance as a racehorse?

The decision is a difficult one and depends on the breeder's personal outlook. Placed in such a situation, I am inclined to think that much would depend upon whether I liked the mare as a character or not. If I did not, the chances are that she would be culled, on the principle that her presence on the stud, and of foals from her of a similar nature, would afford me no pleasure. But if I was fond of the mare, I would give her a chance, doing my best to correct her shortcoming by selective mating and getting rid of those of her foals that inherited their dam's weakness. If she proved a failure as a broodmare, she would be found a good home or be painlessly destroyed, which is far kinder than selling her at public auction and thus perhaps condemning her to an unhappy fate. While it is impossible to ensure that all one's culls are securely and happily placed, much can be done towards finding a happy medium between abandoning a mare to her fate and incurring considerable financial loss by giving her away. It is sometimes possible to sell a mare for a bit less than she would make at public auction, with the proviso that she is never resold. We have been able to do this on two occasions.

The run-of-the-mill surplus stock has to take its chance in the sale ring, but any old mares or failures are best painlessly destroyed, as it is the cheap lots that are most likely to fall into bad hands. A mare who has done her breeder good service should be retired and kept in comfort until she dies or fails in health, in which case she should be put down. La Paiva was retired at the age of nineteen and had the best of everything that we could give her for her remaining few years. Though there is no reason why she should not have gone on breeding, we felt that she had earned a rest from the exigencies of bearing foals and bringing them up – a decision which was rewarded by her looking half her age and proving a most valuable governess to weaned foals and yearlings, or as a companion to maiden or barren mares. To see a good old mare worn out by bearing foals into old age, her joints on the ground and the years showing in her looks and demeanour is a sad sight.

If the stock on the stud as a whole show signs of deterioration, despite the stallions used being successful ones and the mares having no apparent flaw, the chances are that there is something wrong with the land, water, feeding or general management, and the breeder should go into all these aspects with a tooth-comb. Sometimes, if the water is supplied from the mains, the source may be changed, unknown to the user, so the calcium content may have dropped; or the corn may have been affected by contact with some harmful substance; or the land have become stale through having had horses on it for too many years, in which case it will need a rest if it is ever to produce good results again. Some breeders faced with the problem of their stock deteriorating have dealt successfully with it by arranging to send the weaned foals to an entirely different environment, for instance Ireland, keeping them there till they go into training. Naturally, for such a change of environment to prove of the greatest benefit, the stud to which the weanlings are sent must be on good land, well managed and not over-horsed.

Continuity of success in a stud depends on the breeder keeping a critical eye on the rise and fall in racing merit, soundness, constitution, temperament and general appearance of his stock. To delude himself that his geese are swans is the prelude to disaster; and while he should not panic if he has a couple of bad years – which can be the outcome of circumstances, such as virus in the stable in which his horses are trained – he must face the issue when unmistakable signs of deterioration become evident.

Environment

Of all the aspects of Thoroughbred breeding, I believe that in the long-run environment is one of the most important, if not *the* most important.

Environment covers not only pasture, climate and geographical situation, but stud management, feeding, handling of stock, stabling, water and the ambience of the stud farm.

Only by environment does it seem possible to account for horses of top international calibre being produced from second-class exported stock. Physical changes due to environmental changes are an established fact and are sometimes evident in an individual moved from one environment to an entirely different one, as with the stock of exported horses. New factors seem to be introduced so that an outcross involving stock raised in widely differing environments represents a sharper contrast and, in consequence, gives more hybrid vigour than an outcross formed by crossing unrelated stock reared in the same environment.

Improvement evident in stock sent to a fresh environment may be due to factors which were not present in the previous environment.

The importance of water has been underlined earlier: if the water does not contain the necessary calcium, the stock will suffer in faulty and unsound limbs. Unsuitable or badly farmed pastures can also have a detrimental effect.

One reason why some Thoroughbreds thrive abroad is that certain individuals need more sunshine than others. The origin of the Thoroughbred is chiefly oriental, the cornerstone of the breed being the Arabian horse, reared in the desert in a hot, dry climate. Most horses thrive in heat rather than cold, though dry cold does not affect them in the same way as damp cold or incessant rain, which they dislike. On Harry Oppenheimer's Mauritzfontein Stud at Kimberley in South Africa, where the heat can be intense, I have noticed horses choosing to stay in the sun rather than in the shade. Ribofilio (Ribot–Island Creek, by Khaled), who stood at his stud, simply loved the heat, and though provided with shade in his paddock, always preferred to be in the sun, however hot. It is an interesting fact that most of the stock of Ribot do not produce their best racing form until mid-summer.

The desert environment, devoid of lush pasture, produces hard, tough bone of an ivory-like texture; what it lacks in quantity it makes up in quality. This is an important point in a racehorse, since the heavier the frame, the more effort is required to propel it. Whereas the necessary substance of bone is essential, the quality of the bone is more important, and horses reared on overlush pastures, which are ideal for fattening cattle and producing a good milk yield, tend to grow too much and too soft bone.

Care of pastures

Discovering the suitability of pasture is sometimes a matter of trial and error, but however good a pasture may be naturally, it will not give the best results unless it is properly farmed. Above all, it must not be allowed to become horse-sick through being overstocked or because of neglect in lifting the horse-droppings. Horses are terrible foulers of land and unless paddocks are kept clean, grazed with bullocks and not over-horsed, the stock reared on them will deteriorate. That horses can be dosed for red-worm, which is sometimes offered as an excuse for not lifting the droppings, does not alter the fact that continued grazing by horses of paddocks from which the droppings are not lifted makes them horse-sick.

Only if the extent of pasture is huge, the number of horses grazed on it is small in proportion to the number of bullocks, and the land is periodically rested from horses altogether can there be little or no risk of it becoming horse-sick if the droppings are not removed.

The basic reason for not lifting the droppings on paddocks is that it is too much trouble and, in terms of man hours, too expensive, but so far as breeding good horses is concerned this is false economy. Nowadays it is possible to remove droppings by means of a kind of agricultural vacuum cleaner; this is more effective and less severe on the grass than the old method of doing it by hand with a spade.

Breeders who do not have the droppings picked up will point to winners bred in spite of their neglecting to do so. The answer to this is: 'Would not the winners be more numerous and of better quality if the paddocks were kept clean?' To see the amount of droppings picked up in a day from paddocks with only two or three horses on them is a formidable sight and gives some idea of what over-horsed paddocks, from which the droppings are never lifted, must be like.

All this points to the advisability of having a small number of mares in relation to the acreage of pasture available, keeping the paddocks clean and well grazed by bullocks, and concentrating on quality rather than quantity, if the object is to breed good racehorses, as opposed merely to making money out of boarders.

That horses appreciate clean paddocks is evident by the way in which, on over-horsed paddocks, they tend to put down their droppings in one area, leaving at least some part of the ground clean.

Another disadvantage of leaving the droppings on the paddocks is that where they fall the grass grows in thick, coarse clumps, often thickly interspersed with nettles, thistles and dock-leaves, which the horses will not touch. Cattle can be encouraged to eat these clumps by sprinkling them with agricultural salt, but even so their presence means less grazing for the horses.

While many weeds, such as dandelions, are palatable and beneficial to horses, docks, nettles and ragwort are not, and should be removed either by spraying, pulling up in the case of docks and ragwort, or cutting down in the case of thistles and nettles. If spraying is resorted to, hormone and not poison sprays should be used: the less chemistry that is put on horse pasture, the better. Ragwort is an even worse menace, since if left to die on the ground and eaten by cattle or horses it is poisonous. Luckily, it is easy to pull up by hand and with its bright yellow flower can be seen without difficulty.

Thistles are not harmful. In fact, when they are dead and have dried up horses and cattle will eat them, but since horses do not like grazing close to them or going through them, because of being pricked, they are no asset to paddocks as they take up grazing ground and make foals and yearlings lift their legs like hackneys instead of developing a racehorse's action. This may be of minor significance, but is not a desirable trend. Continued cutting weakens and gradually gets rid of thistles, but it is a waste of time cutting them before July, except for the sake of appearance, as they only grow again. If cut from July onward, thistles are finished for the year.

Buttercups sour the land and are disliked by horses. They can be kept under control by mowing or spraying.

It is remarkable how much can be done by cutting down nettles, buttercups, etc., merely by carrying round a hand cutter when walking over the stud and by pulling up ragwort and docks when coming across them. If the stud groom, studmen and breeder himself make a habit of this procedure it is a great help in keeping obnoxious weeds under control.

When we took over the East Woodhay House Stud, the paddocks had been greatly neglected and I must have pulled up acres of ragwort and cut down innumerable patches of thistles and nettles. By this means, and spraying one paddock for thistles, another for buttercups, we got them under control in a surprisingly short time, but all aspects of keeping paddocks in good order requires continuous vigilance and work. If stud paddocks are in bad condition it is because of ignorance, lack of sufficient labour or bad management.

Everyone has his own ideas about management of pasture; mine are based on observation of the paddocks on other studs, both good and bad, listening to experts who have proved their ideas by successful results and by trial and error.

Of one thing I am convinced: paddocks should only be ploughed up and reseeded as a last resort, and reseeded paddocks should not be grazed by bloodstock until at least three years after they have been resown. Shortly after the war there was a craze for reseeding paddocks and putting young stock on them more or less straight away. This had disastrous results in producing horses with bad legs. It is a far better proposition to resuscitate a paddock by rest, grazing with cattle, if necessary limeing and slagging and judicious mowing, than to plough and reseed.

The procedure adopted on our own stud, which seemed to give good results, was as follows.

Paddocks to be used for grazing, as opposed to those being rested, were not mown until the horses and cattle had eaten them down. The reason for this is that the horses like eating the heads of the grass which, if the grass is kept topped, are not available. In its natural state, grassland is not mown and the nearer a breeder can keep to nature, within reason, the better his results are likely to be. Another method is to mow the paddock, leaving an unmown strip under the rails, which the horses can get at, thereby keeping the area tidy.

As a rule the horses and bullocks run together. It is usual for cattle on a stud to be dehorned, but this precaution is probably not essential, as cattle and horses run amicably together and I have never known one of the bullocks on our stud attack a mare, foal or yearling. On the contrary, it is the horses who are most likely to chivvy the bullocks, some of them taking especial delight in cutting out a particular bullock and chasing him across the paddock. One advantage of running cattle with horses is that they help to keep the flies off the horses, who will often get in amongst the bullocks for this purpose, or single out a bullock and follow him round, using his tail to keep the flies off their faces. By running bullocks with the horses, the paddocks are kept sweeter than when grazed by horses only, since they eat the coarser grass, do not carry red-worm and their droppings, when harrowed in, are good for the land.

After the horses have had enough of a paddock, which they indicate by their general mien and appearance – it is easier to sense than to describe – they should be moved to a fresh paddock, the cattle being left to eat it down until there is no more for them to take off (they will show this by becoming restless and trying to get at the grass beyond the paddock rails). Then the cattle are moved to another paddock, the remaining rough grass being taken off with the mower and the paddock harrowed both ways. In about a fortnight, depending upon the rain, the paddock will have a fresh, new growth and can be grazed again when required, the procedure being repeated. If a paddock is not to be grazed again until the following season, it should be topped regularly, the grass being kept fairly short, so that the clippings are not long enough to form lumps on the surface. Before the end of the season it must again be harrowed each way and rolled, and again the following year, about February or March, according to the weather.

All the time the horses are grazing, the droppings should be lifted regularly, twice or three times a week according to the number of horses on the paddock; and when the horses and cattle have been taken off, the paddock ought to be gone over carefully to ensure that all the horse droppings have been removed before harrowing takes place. We seldom had more than one horse to eight or ten acres, and usually not more than four in a paddock, so that it was not necessary to pick up the droppings daily so long as the paddock was thoroughly cleaned after the horses were taken out of it.

It is not advisable to put chemical fertilizers on the paddocks; the only dressing they need is limeing and slagging every few years.

In the past I once dressed the paddocks with fish manure; the result was quite good, but it seemed to encourage the growth of too much clover, which can be an embarrassment on a stud and is not easy to control. Another two-edged experiment was dressing with liquid seaweed. It produced a wonderful growth, and horses relished it, but it proved too rich, resulting in bony enlargements appearing in the stock.

On the subject of cattle, it is wise to have only bullocks on a stud, not cows or heifers, since the latter pose the danger of introducing brucellosis (contagious abortion), which plays havoc with mares.

The time of year at which cattle arrive and leave a stud depends upon the weather and the type of soil on the stud. In wet weather or on heavy land cattle can cause a good deal of damage, albeit temporarily, by poaching the ground if introduced too early or kept too late. It is a matter of regulating their stay according to circumstances.

All this needs constant vigilance and thought, watching how horses, pasturage and cattle are reacting and according to their behaviour doing what seems to be to the best advantage. It is a combination of knowledge, experience, trial and error, intelligent observation and agricultural and horse sense. Conditions on different studs demand different procedures; it is important for the breeder to know his stud thoroughly and determine how it can be farmed to give the best results.

One way of getting paddocks eaten down and cleaned up is to run sheep on them. They graze the grass very closely and destroy parasites and they are of particular benefit on bad pasturage or at the end of a season on a paddock that is to be rested for the winter. However, I have always been brought up never to have sheep on the paddocks, a view expressed by the late Harry Sharpe in *The Practical Stud Groom*. Sheep do a good cosmetic job, but they do not benefit the paddocks as regards horses as do bullocks. Other points against sheep are that, unlike cattle, they do not combat red-worm, and if left too long on a paddock they eat the grass down to the roots, allowing weeds to take over and choke the growth of the young grass.

Management of stock

The first essential in the management of horses on a stud farm is good personnel. There is no quicker or easier way to ruin a horse, especially a highly-strung Thoroughbred, than by wrong handling, whether at the stud or in a racing stable. If a horse has a bad start to life because of ignorant and unsympathetic treatment as a foal or yearling, his whole future may be affected adversely, while the unfortunate staff of the racing stable to which he is consigned are going to have a difficult time with him.

Therefore it is of paramount importance that the staff on a stud farm should understand and like horses, treating them with patience, sympathy and, at the same time, not be afraid of them.

I have known yearlings arrive at a racing stable as, literally, wild animals. This is inexcusable and breeders who send them into training in such a state have no moral right to be in the business. It means that their staff are no good, or are overworked or that the owner or manager is at fault, which goes for most causes of failure, be it in government, business or breeding racehorses.

The best stud groom and staff in the world cannot do their job properly if they have too many horses to look after, and a breeder who permits such a situation either does not know what he is about or is trying to run his business on the cheap, in which case he is better occupied in some other sphere.

Racing and breeding are costly pursuits and so far as the owner-breeder is concerned better results are to be achieved by a small, well-run enterprise than one too large for its resources. Likewise, an owner-breeder boarding his mares out is likely to be better served by placing them at a stud where quality comes before quantity, even if it costs more.

The earlier a horse's education begins, the easier will his lessons come to him. The sooner a head-collar is put on a foal and he is taught to lead, the more smoothly will the first steps have been taken. The more he is handled in the first few weeks of his life, the better for the foal and for those who have to deal with him later. When a foal returns home with his dam after she has visited a stallion, it is possible to tell in a few minutes how well or badly he has been handled. On the whole, I would say that all bloodstock is more sympathetically and intelligently handled than was the case fifty years ago, when accidents to foals and yearlings were not uncommon because they were often not handled properly before being broken, and savage horses in racing stables and among stallions were part of the general scene.

When our foals returned to the studs at which they had been for their dams to be covered, they were taught by stages to submit to being brushed over, have their eyes, noses and docks sponged out, and their feet picked out before they went out in the morning. Since we were fortunate enough for the mares visiting stallions at Newmarket to be able to stay at the Egerton Stud, one of the best-run in the country, the foals were well handled from the day of their birth and presented no problems when it came to furthering their education. They soon learned to stand without being held while they were being got ready to go out.

The mares and foals went out after being brushed over, etc., at 7.30 a.m. and stayed out, wet or fine, sunshine or snow, until dusk. Our paddocks were well sheltered and surrounded by trees, the park paddock also having trees in it, so that the horses had protection when it was wet. While horses seek the shelter of trees when it rains they do not seem to like going into sheds to do so, though they enter them in hot weather. I do not know the reason for this – perhaps they dislike the rattle of the rain on the roof – but it indicates that it is desirable to have the shelter of trees available in paddocks, as well as hedges to provide a break from the wind.

Since we seldom had more than two mares and their foals in one paddock, it was no problem feeding them out. Each mare and foal shared a bin and, if given to knocking it over, the feed was put on the ground. None was wasted and though in making sure of this the horses left almost bald patches, these soon grew up again. If the mare was greedy and made it difficult for the foal to get its share, the latter had its own feed some yards away. Over the years, the system worked efficiently.

When there were too many mares and foals to be fed in the paddock, they were brought in at midday, fed and turned out again. While out, the foals were regularly handled and talked to (which all horses appreciate greatly) so that they did not forget their early lessons. We once had a German mare who appreci-ated being talked to in her home tongue.

It is a great help to his eventual breaking-in to accustom a foal to wearing a roller or strap at an early stage and to get used to having a bit in his mouth. By this method, and constant handling, we found that it was easy to progress to putting a saddle on his back and riding him round the box before he went into training.

When yearlings have been brought to this stage of education, trainers are happy to receive them, though otherwise unbroken, since they do not present any problem when the usual breaking tackle is put on them. Brigadier Gerard was broken on the stud, partly for reasons of economy, but he was the only yearling on the place at the time. As a general rule we did not break the yearlings entirely, as there was so much other work to do on the stud.

In the old days, tacking yearlings when they arrived at a racing stable was often akin to breaking a mustang straight off the prairie. Many had never had any form of tack on them other than a head-collar, had received little handling and when tacked for the first time plunged and threw themselves about in frustration and terror, sometimes doing themselves serious, even fatal, injury. If a yearling showed plenty of fight, it was regarded as a sign that he was tough and courageous. More gradual and intelligent handling does nothing to diminish a horse's courage, but reduces the chance of accidents and does not cause him to lose confidence in human nature.

How stock is brought up on a stud depends to a certain extent on the geographical and climatic conditions in which the stud is situated. On a stud where paddocks have no shelter whatsoever and the climate is severe, Thoroughbreds will not thrive whether they run out night and day in all weather or are brought in at night. The nub of the matter is that if conditions do not permit horses to run out night and day from about May to October, the stud is not suitable for breeding racehorses. Provided that horses are well fed, have sheltered paddocks and are not up to their knees and hocks in mud, the more they are out the better. One winter we ran four in-foal mares out day and night until they went off to be covered the following spring. It was a dry winter, but bitterly cold, up to 32° of frost. All did well and had healthy foals, one being La Paiva's first foal, The Travellers (by Gratitude), who won four races; two of the others won and the remaining one was placed. In other districts, where mares were being kept in for weeks on end with no exercise, a number had deformed foals. My mares were very highly fed and looked well, so much so that when La Paiva went to the National Stud to be covered by Big Game they would not believe that she had been out all winter.

In places such as Australia and Florida it is customary to run horses out the whole year round, the climate being suited to this procedure, and horses do well on it, Australian horses being particularly tough. The disadvantage of this system in England is the climate, chiefly the wet, since pure cold presents little problem. However, the breeding and racing of horses for the flat is an artificial operation, since they are required to run as two-year-olds, several years before they would reach their full development in a natural state. This entails a different approach from the one designed by nature. Firstly, they must be highly fed and secondly a happy medium between coddling and a spartan upbringing must be found. Their development should not be retarded by having to use up most of the energy supplied by their food in keeping themselves warm; on the other hand, unless running out for sufficiently long periods, preferably all summer and from early morning till dusk for the rest of the year, their heart, lungs, tendons, sinews and muscles will not grow and toughen as they ought to do.

At all times the top halves of the doors of the loose boxes are best kept open. If the weather is exceptionally bad, the top door may be kept half-open. In *The Practical Stud Groom*, Harry Sharpe quotes the case of Thoroughbred horses in Canada running with half-bred horses on the range and fending for themselves. The Thoroughbreds soon adapted themselves and thrived in natural conditions, but grew smaller than would have been the case if artificially reared. On the same basis, horses bred essentially to race over fences and who run out all the year round, without being corn fed, take a long time to come to hand and as steeplechasers often do not reach their prime until they are nine years old.

Thus, in breeding flat racers, the happy medium would seem to be the most satisfactory method in England. That is, running all the horses out night and day from about the end of May to the beginning of October and from 7.30 a.m. to dusk for the remainder of the year – in all weathers. The system presents certain problems where the workers live some way from the stud itself, since for part of the year it entails their coming back at about 8 or 9 o'clock at night. On our own stud, matters were simplified by everything being on a small scale and the stud groom and studmen living close by on the place. The working hours were adjusted accordingly and there was usually an extra man available in myself, if one was required. The system proved agreeable to everyone and since it is more likely to produce good racehorses than one which entails bringing the horse in at about 3 o'clock in the afternoon, it is to the eventual benefit of all.

The more fresh air horses get, the freer they are from germs. My own stud groom, who graduated via old-fashioned, orthodox studs, where foals and yearlings were never left out day and night and the horses were brought in at the first sign of rain, on several occasions observed to me how much healthier and freer from dirty noses were our own young stock, compared with those brought up under less robust conditions.

To bring horses in at night during the summer is contrary to nature, since it is at night that they like to graze, wandering about in the cool, while during the day they doze and sun themselves. If horses are pampered too much, they do not learn to look after themselves or stand up to adverse conditions. To bring them in or not turn them out at all because it is raining is sheer nonsense; if unaccustomed to being out in the rain, they will be disinclined to face it on the racecourse and, in consequence, fail to give their best running, which might mean defeat instead of victory in a major race. La Paiva and all her foals had exceptionally fine coats and loathed rain, but learned to put up with it so that they were not affected by it on the racecourse. This was borne out in the Champion Stakes of 1971, in which Brigadier Gerard had to race in pouring rain and, despite heavy going, which was a great disadvantage to him, he battled on to victory.

Like wet, a vexed problem is that of flies in hot weather. One school of thought is that when the flies are bad, the horses should be brought in during the day and turned out at night. We tried this, also leaving them out in spite of the flies and, on the basis that they will have to put up with flies on the racecourse and training ground and that it is part of nature to do so, I think that in the long run it is best to let them learn to live with them. By herding together, or among the cattle, they keep the flies under control and in general do not seem unduly worried by them. Some breeders attach fringes to the head collars that come over the horses' faces, but we always removed the head collars, as it is more comfortable for the horses without them. This practice would not, however, be wise on a large stud, where there are visiting mares, since identities might get mixed up.

No part of breeding has aroused more controversy than that of weaning. Some breeders advocate early weaning, others late. There is the school that favours separating mare and foal in one fell swoop, those who prefer gradual weaning.

The theory behind early weaning is that it lessens the burden on an in-foal mare because she does not have to feed the foal at foot, at the same time supporting the one she is carrying. In favour of late weaning is that it is less of a shock to the weaned foal, mentally and physically, as a result of which the foal does not lose condition after weaning.

My preference is for late weaning, which is nearer to nature and, in my experience, has no detrimental effect on the mare but is beneficial to the foal. To see a group of foals who have just been weaned at an early age is a sad sight, rather akin to tearful small boys who have been sent straight from the comforts of home to a boarding-school at the age of six. Miserable in demeanour, tucked-up in condition, they stand around in a bunch, bewildered and apprehensive of what is next in store for them. Foals weaned later, and gradually, accept the separation from their dams almost without a qualm; each has got rather tired of the other and after a couple of days at the most have put each other out of mind. In our experience, mares whose foals are weaned late suffer in no way whatsoever; as the foals grow up, they become less and less interested in their dams' milk, so do not bother them with undue attention in this respect. Whether this disinterest would be as marked, and the effect on the mare be so unharmful, if mare and foal were not corn fed, I cannot say, since our mares and foals were fed all the time they were running out.

The system of weaning which we evolved by trial and error and found to be eminently satisfactory is as follows. The weaning starts when the foals are approximately six months old; of two foals who are to run together, one will probably be a bit older than the other, and since we liked to start the weaning not earlier than mid-September, so that the mares and foals were out night and day as long as possible, foals may be older or younger than six months when the time for their weaning arrives.

On the first day, when the mare and foal were brought in for the night, they were put in adjoining boxes with between them an open grille through which they could see each other. In the past we kept them thus for a week and then, in the morning, separated them completely, putting the foals in one paddock and the mares in another, as far apart as possible. Later, we tried a further refinement, with even better results. After the first week, we kept them in adjoining boxes for a further week, but with the grille closed. This entailed a longer and more definite, but not complete, separation and when the mare and foal were parted completely they settled down even more quickly than before.

On a small stud, there are sometimes occasions when there is only one foal on the place. Thus arises the problem of finding a companion for it. Sometimes one can borrow a foal from a friend; on other occasions the companion may be a hunter or a pony. Brigadier Gerard ran with a pony, to whom he became extremely attached; but this gave rise to an unforeseen problem when he went into training, since the sight of any pony upset him greatly, as he thought it might be his old friend. His half-brother, Brigade Major (Major Portion–La Paiva), ran with a Thoroughbred ex-chaser called South Grove, to whom he was devoted. No emotional repercussion resulted and the racing record of the two half-brothers is proof of the success of the operation: Brigadier Gerard's achievements are well known, while Brigade Major won the Kempton Park Great Jubilee Handicap, the Cosmopolitan Cup and a valuable maiden race.

Trainers have told me that they have found yearlings who have run with an older horse to be more sensible and mature in demeanour than those who have had only the company of fellow yearlings. Likewise, a retired broodmare forms an excellent governess for yearling fillies. Needless to say, it is important that the older gelding or mare should have a kind and equable temperament. This being the case, they have the patience to put up with such youthful tricks as having their tails pulled or being nipped surreptitiously, at the same time possessing the strength and authority to keep the yearlings in order.

When an older gelding or mare is to keep a single weaned foal company, he or she is put in the adjoining box to the foal, with the grille open, when the mare is taken away. Sometimes the older horse may be run with the mare and foal for a week or so, to enable the foal to get to know his or her future companion before the mare is removed.

Thus a retired broodmare and gelding, provided they have a suitable temperament, are valuable assets on a small stud.

When the weather is warm enough towards the end of May, the yearlings, as they then are, can run out night and day with their companions until the time comes for the former to go into training. Some breeders turn them out earlier in the year, in April, and so long as they are well fed the exact date of the change is probably immaterial. Others leave them until later, in the hope of the weather having reached a reasonable degree of consistency, since horses react unfavourably to violent changes of temperature, as do humans.

Foals and yearlings should be wormed periodically, depending on whether tests of the droppings indicate the advisability of this, or their appearance – a pot belly and staring coat – suggests their need of this treatment. The necessity of the owner or manager keeping a sharp eye on the running of the stud in general is indicated by the experience of one breeder in the matter of worming. He could not understand why, without fail, each test showed every horse on the stud to have a nil count of worms. This seemed too good to be true, as it is virtually impossible to avoid at least a minute count to appear in some foal or yearling, even on the best-managed studs. The breeder eventually discovered that, in order to make himself appear super-efficient, the stud groom had been sending up the droppings to be tested immediately after the horses had been wormed.

While it is essential to keep a close watch on young stock to keep them free from worms, the less they have to be dosed for anything the better. Likewise, unless a horse is seriously ill or has an infection that persists, the use of antibiotics is best avoided as the time may come when they are really needed and they may not have the desired effect. Modern veterinary science, like modern medicine, tends to fly to drugs at the drop of a hat, however trivial the complaint, and apart from the expense of such not always essential medical niceties, the further horses – and humans – can be kept away from them, the better for each in the long run.

In recent years a most dangerous practice has crept into racing and breeding, to say nothing of athletics – the use of anabolic steroids. These advance the growth and development of horses unnaturally and in terms of early two-year-olds and three-year-olds, as well as sale yearlings, may pay short-term dividends, but are extremely dangerous in that they can affect the fertility of horses and mares who have been thus treated, when they go to stud. Besides, they give a false impression of true racing ability, so that a breeder cannot assess accurately the material with which he is dealing. I heard of a case of an owner whose trainer asked him if he would be prepared to have his horse treated with anabolic steroids, as he thought that by that means the horse's condition could be greatly improved, adding that he had a couple of two-year-olds in the yard who had reacted most favourably to the treatment. The owner in question said he would think it over and let him know; meanwhile he consulted an eminent veterinary surgeon, who told him to have nothing to do with them. The owner informed the trainer, who shortly afterwards sent the horse back. Not long afterwards, the matter of anabolic steroids burst on the public through the press, together with the announcement that a method of detecting them in humans had been discovered. Now they can be detected in horses. It was an interesting coincidence that the two-year-olds concerned proved most disappointing the following season, one turning out to be sterile when retired to stud.

Since the owner-breeder is master of his own destiny in that he has to bear the consequences of how he treats his yearlings, he is well advised to keep clear of such aids as anabolic steroids, hormones, etc., on the stud, otherwise he will pay for it in terms of racing performance, as the horses will miss the treatment when they go into training – only a lunatic trainer would risk his licence by using them now – and jeopardize his stud. Commercial breeders are differently placed, since it is someone else's worry once a yearling has been knocked down; but yearling buyers should be careful to buy only from studs which can be relied upon not to use dangerous, artificial aids.

It is essential on a stud to have the services of a good farrier and to have the feet of every horse on the stud looked at once a month. This is particularly important with foals, since deformities such as turning a foot out or in can be improved, even corrected, by a skilled farrier if dealt with early and regularly. The way in which a foal's foot grows can also be influenced by the farrier's attention. English breeders as a whole give far too little care to the matter of horses' feet, not only from the point of view of their treatment, but also in acquiring prospective broodmares and designing matings. Were racing conditions in England as hard on horses as they are in the USA, where a high proportion of horses break down and a number never reach the racecourse at all, feet would become a more important factor than is the case. Even so, an owner-breeder should bear in mind that he will annually have to get rid of surplus stock, both horses in training and, sometimes, mares or fillies; so they must have good feet and legs if they are to appeal to buyers in the USA or countries such as Australia and South Africa, where sound, well-formed feet and legs count for much.

Under the heading of care of stock must come the fencing of paddocks. With the ever-rising cost of timber, the time may come when breeders will have to resort to wire fencing. This may not prove as disastrous a move as it sounds, since horses are adaptable and soon learn to accept new ways. In fact, a successful owner-breeder of the present time, when questioned about the amount of barbed wire on his stud, observed that, as farmers whose land bordered training grounds invariably used a good deal of barbed wire for fencing, it was as well for horses to know all about it in case they got loose on the gallops. Horses running out the whole time are not so liable to get into trouble with fencing as those who are turned out only for an hour or two a day. The former find their way around quietly, while the latter are often too fresh to know or think what they are doing.

Another aspect of fencing is that cattle have a habit of breaking out by smashing rails. By trial and error we discovered that the happy medium is to run one strand of plain wire between the top and second rail and one between the second rail and the ground. This is pretty effective in preventing the cattle from breaking out and does not seem to cause the horses any damage. There are certain horses who seem accident-prone and would contrive to injure themselves in a padded paddock, but fortunately these are the exception. Nevertheless, it is always wise to walk round the fencing regularly, looking for protruding nails, loose wire, broken rails and other hazards pertaining to fencing. Smart studs in the USA and some in Europe have their paddock rails painted white; this looks nice and impresses clients of public studs, but is expensive and for practical purposes is no better than creosote. While an untidy, ill-kept stud is an eye-sore, it should be remembered that it is good, well-farmed pasture, judicious choice of mares, selective mating, correct management and feeding that produces winners, not paint and flower-beds.

13

Feeding

There is one golden rule in feeding, whether it be racehorses, broodmares, yearlings or foals: always give them the best, no matter what it costs. 'That hay's good enough for the visiting mares' is an expression not unknown on studs run on the cheap, but it is a misguided policy if the object of the exercise is to breed winners.

For some reason, there is an idea, quite often encountered, that mares, foals and yearlings do not need more than good grass, except in winter. This may be all right as regards store horses, who are not going to be broken before they are four; but in the case of horses who are going to race as two-year-olds corn-feeding is essential, not only when they are old enough to eat grain, but through their dams when they are being carried. When the grass is at its best, from about April to early June, the corn ration can be cut down, but once the goodness has gone out of the grass the corn ration should be increased. Economizing on feeding is equivalent to putting a stone penalty on the horse as regards racing. If a breeder cannot afford to feed his stock really well, it will be better for him to reduce the number of his mares and feed them properly, or go out of the game.

Horses must be fed as individuals, since they do not all react to feeding in the same way; some need more than others and to over-feed is as bad as to under-feed, as this can cause laminitis, legs to puff up, mares to get too fat inside and digestive troubles. The more time that horses spend out of doors, the less do these troubles occur, since they are moving about gently most of the time, stimulating circulation and digestion.

The fewer chemical additives a horse is given, the better; these are usually substitutes for bad pastures and inferior oats and hay. In the past we have tried vitamin additives, but found that they caused bony enlargements which, though disappearing later, suggested that the additives were 'over-egging the pudding'. By trial and error, we arrived at the diet given below, which is subject to modification, according to circumstances. It is emphasised that feeding must be graded to the nature of the pasture: in some cases over-feeding will cause trouble.

FOALS
Morning 1½ bowls of oats and bran (mixed), damped with hot water (cold in hot weather) or dry, according to the weather and given at 6.30 a.m.

Evening 2 bowls of oats
2 bowls of bran
½ bowl of flaked maize (in winter)
handful of chaff (hay)
handful of linseed cake, damped

YEARLINGS
Morning 2 bowls of oats and bran (mixed), damped if desirable (as in the case of the foals)

Evening 2½ bowls of oats
3 bowls of bran
double handful of chaff (hay)
double handful of linseed cake, damped

IN-FOAL MARES
Morning 2 bowls of oats and bran (mixed), damped if desirable
Evening 3 bowls of oats
4 bowls of bran
double handful of chaff (hay)
double handful of linseed cake, damped

BARREN MARES
Morning Heaped bowl of oats and bran
Evening 2 bowls of oats
2 bowls of bran
double handful of chaff
handful of linseed cake, damped

The oats used were the best Australian; these and Canadian oats, being sun-dried (as opposed to kiln-dried), do not cause kidney trouble, as kiln-dried oats may do. When the horses came in at night, they had a supply of hay in the box.

When the horses were out night and day and the grass was at its best, they had only the main feed; when the grass went off, they had the usual two feeds.

In the winter, the horses got a bran mash once a week, but we found that by feeding linseed cake, broken up, the same result was achieved, namely, a healthy coat and loose skin. Some trainers feed linseed cake to racehorses with good results. One advantage of this form of feeding to racehorses, who normally have mashes twice a week, is that it prevents a horse from realizing that something is up when he does not have his mid-week mash because he is running the next day. This can cause a highly-strung horse to fret in anticipation of his race the following day.

While not believing in chemical additives, all the horses got an egg-cupful of apple-cider vinegar in the main feed and the weaned foals and yearlings got an egg-cupful of powdered limestone. The theory behind this is that apple-cider vinegar is reputedly a virus-killer – the horses certainly enjoy it and it appears to keep them healthy – while the powdered limestone is supposed to help the growth and quality of bone. Whether this has anything to do with it or not, our young stock grew good bone.

Like every other aspect of stud management, good feeding depends upon careful observation of the individual and modification of diet according to circumstances.

If a horse does not thrive on the diet outlined, provided the feed is of the highest quality, there is something wrong with him, or he has such a weak constitution that he is not worth keeping.

Should the weather become exceptionally severe, or if horses are ever run out night and day in winter, the ration must be stepped up and flaked maize added to the diet of the older ones.

It cannot be over-emphasised that in all aspects of feeding racehorses, be they mares, foals, yearlings, stallions or horses in training, only the best is good enough.

14

Planning for Racing

The most promising-looking and well-bred yearling may prove useless, but in the hope he may turn out to be up to classic standard, it is as well to have a programme in mind for him. It may need modifying, or scrapping altogether, according to circumstances, but it is an entertaining diversion during the winter months and oils the wheels of race planning should the horse fulfil his owner's highest hopes. Here is a hypothetical example.

The horse, X, is a February foal, well made and well grown, and has a classic 10–14-furlong pedigree. Physically he gives the impression that he will come to hand sufficiently early to win as a two-year-old, if good enough, but would benefit from not being raced until June at the earliest.

At two years
Choice of his first race would be influenced by the following: the proximity of the course to his stable; the likelihood of good going; not too big a field – standing in the stalls for ten minutes or so, waiting for the last of 27 runners to be got in does not help a highly-strung two-year-old first time out; not too formidable opposition; the time of year; his state of fitness.

In selecting a race it is worth looking up the details of the previous two or three years' running to get an idea of the general trend governing it: races seem to follow a remarkably consistent pattern as regards the number of runners and the quality of the contestants.

In this case a suitable debut for a horse trained within a reasonable distance from this course would seem to be the Champagne Stakes in late June, at Salisbury over six furlongs.

It conforms to the requirements noted above, being close to the training stable, usually run on going without any jar, attracting about six runners and excluding the good two-year-olds running at Royal Ascot the previous week.

Assuming, albeit optimistically, that the horse proves good

enough to follow a top-level programme throughout his racing career, his next appearance might be the July Stakes at Newmarket, over six furlongs in the second week of July, followed by the Gimcrack Stakes at York, six furlongs, in the third week of August.

At this point there must be a pause for reflection in the light of the type and class of performer the horse has shown himself to be. If, despite his pedigree, he has given every indication of being able to cope with top-class horses at six furlongs, the Middle Park would be his best main target for the season and he would not appear again until then. This is a Group I race run at Newmarket in early October over six furlongs.

If, on the other hand, the horse would seem not quite fast enough to cope with the best of his rivals over this distance, the Dewhurst Stakes, over seven furlongs at Newmarket a fortnight later, would be a more suitable objective.

Though not so valuable as the Group I mile race at Doncaster whose name keeps changing, the Dewhurst is a happy medium between the six furlongs of the Middle Park and the mile of the Doncaster race.

While a mile may not be too far for a stoutly bred two-year-old, it can prove an exacting test to a horse of this age in heavy going, especially a top-class horse with good speed and not a true twelve-furlong pedigree. I feel that the shorter distance of the Dewhurst offers a more gradual approach to a three-year-old career than the mile of the Doncaster race. The higher the ability of the horse, the less will he be affected by the choice of the race, since a really good horse is unlikely to be extended; but it is a mistake to prejudice the future of a two-year-old of classic promise through being attracted by the value of a race as opposed to going for a less exacting but more suitable task carrying a smaller prize. The ultimate aim is the classics and the top international Group I races open to older horses, and it is wise to bear this in mind before committing a two-year-old to a race which may not be the one best suited to his particular qualities.

As already noted, much depends upon the type of horse in question; a tough, staying type such as Vaguely Noble is probably better suited to the mile of the Doncaster race than the six furlongs of the Middle Park or even the seven furlongs of the Dewhurst.

My personal inclination is not to run a serious contender for the following year's Two Thousand Guineas beyond six furlongs as a two-year-old. Thus, if the horse in question seems to have the speed for the Middle Park, this becomes the next and last race for him as a juvenile.

On the other hand, should the Dewhurst or the Futurity be his target, he could have a preliminary race in the Group II Mill Reef Stakes about 20 September, over six furlongs at Newbury.

This is a fairly new race which comes too close to the Middle Park for it to be an entirely desirable stepping-stone to that, but is almost a month before the Dewhurst.

At three years

The first consideration in planning a horse's three-year-old career is whether or not he is going to race at four. If so he can be given a rational, but ambitious programme, with intervals between his races which enable him to be produced at his best for each engagement and not be raced too often.

The view has already been expressed that every owner of a top three-year-old who has the true interests of racing and breeding at heart should race him on as a four-year-old. Money is not everything. Or is it?

Thus, so far as the case in question is concerned, the horse's three-year-old career is to be planned with an eye to a season's racing as a four-year-old.

On the assumption that he has given sufficient evidence of being fast enough to merit running in the Two Thousand Guineas, this would be his first target.

The longer a horse's first appearance can be delayed, the more he will benefit, because the weather will be getting warmer, and the more likely he is to retain his form to the end of the season. In any case, the races before the Two Thousand Guineas carry little prestige, can represent the chance of a defeat that was not necessary, and can do more harm than good in a cold spring.

Thus, unless he is a sluggish worker at home and really needs a preliminary race, the Two Thousand Guineas (Group I), at the beginning of May, over one mile at Newmarket, becomes the first outing of the horse's three-year-old career. If a preliminary race is considered necessary, I favour the Craven Stakes over the Guineas course.

Should the horse have indicated that he is essentially a Derby–Leger type, a different plan is desirable. Derby winners such as Windsor Lad, Hyperion, Never Say Die and Airborne come into the former category. It would then be preferable to choose a race longer than the Two Thousand Guineas as a preliminary to contesting the Derby.

The most desirable alternatives to my mind are the Chester Vase (Group III), over 1½ miles at the Chester May meeting; the Lingfield Derby Trial (Group III) over 1 mile 3 furlongs; or the Dante Stakes (Group III), run at York over 1¼ miles, both about 12 May.

Fairly recent Derby winners who have succeeded in one or more of these races include Shergar and Henbit in the Chester Vase, Reference Point and Shahastrani in the Dante Stakes, and Slip Anchor and Teenoso in the Lingfield Derby Trial. The choice depends upon circumstances and the nature of the horse. An important factor is the going, since it is not desirable to risk jarring a horse on hard ground or pulling him to pieces in a bog before the Derby.

Some owners and trainers favour the Lingfield race in that it provides a dress rehearsal for Tattenham Hill and Tattenham Corner at Epsom. This is so to a certain extent, but a horse is always more likely to be jarred galloping downhill than on the level, and rather than take this risk, should the ground at Lingfield be hard, it would seem wiser to delay giving the horse a feel of the real thing until he gets to Epsom, letting him have a steady canter down to and round Tattenham Corner the day before or on the morning of the race.

Whether or not to work a horse on the morning of a race must be a matter of trial and error as regards the individual. In the case of the average horse, if he is not fit by the morning of the race, he would be better left at home. On the other hand, to some horses a sharp two furlongs on the morning of a race is absolutely essential: the Rosebery Stakes winner Philadelphe II, who won many other races and was trained by that master of the art the late George Todd, never won unless he had a work-out on the morning of a race. In the case of a particularly high-powered horse, as was Brigadier Gerard, the very fact of being saddled, ridden and hack-cantered on the morning of a race ensured that he would not suffer from over-exuberance in the paddock, thereby becoming open to the chance of getting loose or injuring himself.

Thus, having run at Newmarket, Chester or Lingfield, the horse arrives at Epsom for the Derby. Whatever the outcome, it will be wise to give him at least a month's rest after this race. It should be appreciated that at three years a racehorse is still immature and if he is to finish the season and remain in training at four he must not be over-taxed in his first or second season. This does not mean that he has to be kept in cotton wool, but that he should be given ample time to recover from a top race, particularly the Derby.

This being the case, the choice of the next race lies between the Eclipse Stakes, around 6 July, 1¼ miles at Sandown, and the King George VI and Queen Elizabeth Stakes, around 27 July, 1½ miles at Ascot.

The choice must depend upon circumstances and the philosophy of the owner. That a horse can 'go through the card' in a series of top races, as Grundy did in the Irish Two Thousand, the Derby, the Irish Sweeps Derby (29 June) and the King George VI and Queen Elizabeth Stakes is not disputed, but such a policy is liable to bring its repercussions, as it did with Grundy, who sank in the International Stakes and never surfaced thereafter. However, when the set policy is for the horse to race on as a four-year-old, a less concentrated programme is advisable.

In the event of the horse having shown enough speed to win or nearly win the Two Thousand, my inclination would be to go for the Eclipse, though if there is a good four-year-old in the race, it can be dangerous to take him on with a three-year-old, who is not favoured by weight-for-age at this stage. If, on the other hand, he gave the impression of being a mile-and-a-half-plus horse, the Ascot race would seem preferable.

The lessons of the past are that the International Stakes over 1¼ miles around 20 August at York is a race to avoid with a horse who has contested the King George VI and Queen Elizabeth Stakes. The ideal place in the Calendar for this race is the Doncaster St Leger meeting, where it would provide an excellent preliminary for the Arc de Triomphe or the Champion Stakes and give horses who had run in the King George VI and Queen Elizabeth Stakes, especially three-year-olds, ample time to get over that race. As it is, having proved a graveyard for favourites, owners and trainers have reason to fight shy of the International Stakes with top horses, unless they decide to lay them out specifically for this race.

In the case of X, the International Stakes could be considered if the previous race was the Eclipse, but not if it was the King George VI and Queen Elizabeth Stakes. Presuming the latter to be the case, and the horse to be a Derby–Leger (or triple crown) type, the St Leger would become the next aim. The International Stakes would probably be missed out, as a few weeks' holiday in August would benefit the horse, thus allowing plenty of time for a gradual preparation. If a pre-St Leger race is thought desirable, the Voltigeur Stakes at the York Ebor meeting fits the bill.

The St Leger is a maligned race, having incurred the censure of the critics because the counter-attraction of the Arc de Triomphe has kept a number of good horses away. In fact, it seldom results in a dull race, is less open to fluke results than the Arc de Triomphe, being run on a better course and sounder going than Longchamp provides, and is the oldest classic in the Calendar, which means something to some owners.

Run over fourteen furlongs at Doncaster in the second week of September, the St Leger comes a fortnight before the Arc de Triomphe and just over a month before the Champion Stakes. The huge prize of the Arc has caused more than one owner to be carried away and lose his judgement in running a Leger horse at Longchamp. Nijinsky nearly got away with it, but he was considered an exceptional horse and in the end got beaten, albeit unluckily, as he had a bad run and his jockey lost his whip.

This outlines the value of being able to plan with a four-year-old career in mind, in which case the Arc can be passed over till the following season and, instead, the Champion Stakes over 1¼ miles at Newmarket in October can be made the final objective of the season. This is a race of prestige and a fine test which has produced many great horses among its winners, including those outstanding Leger winners Pretty Polly, Bayardo and Fairway (who won the Champion Stakes twice).

A horse who can get through three full seasons racing in the top class and emerge sound, maintaining his form and with his temperament unimpaired, can be said to have passed every test that can be expected of a flat racer. From the breeder's point of view, it has been possible to assess him from all aspects; his faults and qualities are there for all to see.

At four years

If the horse has got as far as his third season, his racing programme can be stepped up. He will have gained in strength, constitution and confidence, so that racing and travelling will take less out of him, and once he is fit he will probably enjoy earning his keep on the racecourse more than galloping at home. Thus the intervals between some of his races can be lessened without risk of detriment, unless he has had an unusually severe battle.

With this in mind, race planning becomes more elastic. If X has progressed according to the hopes held out for him, my feeling would be to run him in either the Brigadier Gerard Stakes, over 1¼ miles at Sandown around 27 May, or the Coronation Cup, over 1½ miles around 7 June at Epsom, or both. Unless the going seemed likely to be too hard, the Coronation Cup, a valuable, historic race of great prestige, would be first choice. Being a four-year-old (and since the Coronation Cup is never so gruelling a race as the Derby), the horse could quite well go on to Royal Ascot for his next engagement. This might be the Prince of Wales's Stakes over 1¼ miles, the Hardwicke Stakes over 1½ miles or the Ascot Gold Cup, their value being in reverse order. Before the war, every ambitious owner would have decided upon the Ascot Gold Cup; indeed Sir Humphrey de Trafford made this choice with his St Leger winner, Alcide, who was narrowly beaten in the race due to firm ground, but went on to win the King George VI and Queen Elizabeth Stakes – a bold and commendable policy.

With the modern championship distance firmly established at one and a half miles, my feeling would be to concentrate on trying to win the top races at this distance and, like the late Lord Derby with Fairway, leave the Ascot Gold Cup as a five-year-old target, if it was decided to go for it at all. In fact, Lord

Derby's plan never materialized, owing to Fairway showing signs of leg trouble and being taken out of training.

On the assumption that X could cope as well with twelve furlongs as with ten, the Hardwicke Stakes seems the best race for him to tackle next.

His final aim of the season would be a second Champion Stakes or the Arc de Triomphe, the immediate problem being the races in between. Had he won the Eclipse the previous year instead of going for the King George VI and Queen Elizabeth Stakes, it would be more important for him to succeed in the latter – in my view the best race in the world, because it is run at the height of the season when horses are at their peak, as opposed to the Arc de Triomphe, when many have trained off. The Ascot race has never been won by a bad horse, which is not the case with the Arc, while the course is a fairer and truer test than the Longchamp equivalent.

However, there is no reason why a horse should not win both the Eclipse and the King George VI and Queen Elizabeth Stakes in the same year, as did Tulyar, Ballymoss, Busted, Royal Palace, Mill Reef, Brigadier Gerard, Nashwan and Generous, all at four years except Tulyar, Mill Reef, Nashwan and Generous, who were three-year-olds.

With a horse whose aim is the Prix de l'Arc de Triomphe, and who does not contest the International Stakes at York, it will be necessary to give him a preliminary race before he goes to Longchamp. There is no ideally placed race in England for this purpose, the Cumberland Lodge Stakes over 1½ miles at Ascot around 26 September being rather too near the Arc (early October); but a suitable one presents itself at Longchamp, the Prix Foy, over eleven furlongs around 15 September. This has the added attraction of giving a horse experience of all but the first furlong of the Prix de l'Arc de Triomphe course, which is worth quite a bit.

Whether or not a horse races again after the Arc is a matter of personal choice and circumstance. Should he have had a reasonably easy race, have come out of it well and be a tough horse who is a good traveller, the Champion Stakes provides an attractive finale. But the Arc is not an event in which a horse is likely to have an easy race, win, lose or draw; the tempo from start to finish is terrific and, mentally and physically, takes more out of a horse than is evident. My own feeling is that if I were fortunate enough to win the Arc I would call it a day and let the horse down, preparatory to retiring him to stud. He would have earned his retirement.

Thus the schedule of X's three seasons' programme would come out as follows (the dates being approximate and the titles devoid of sponsors' prefixes):

At two years	26 June	Champagne Stakes, Salisbury, 6f.
	10 July	July Stakes, Newmarket, 6f.
	21 August	Gimcrack Stakes, York, 6f.
	21 September	(if Dewhurst Stakes the objective) Mill Reef Stakes, Newbury, 6f.
		or
	3 October	Middle Park Stakes, Newmarket, 6f.
	18 October	Dewhurst Stakes, Newmarket, 7f. (if not started for the Middle Park)
At three years	16 April	Craven Stakes, Newmarket, 1 mile (only if previous race is required)
	2 May	Two Thousand Guineas, Newmarket, 1 mile
		or
	7 May	Chester Vase, Chester, 1½ miles
		or
	11 May	Derby Trial Stakes, Lingfield, 1 mile, 3f.
		or
	12 May	Dante Stakes, York, 1¼ miles
	5 June	The Derby, Epsom, 1½ miles
	6 July	Eclipse Stakes, Sandown, 1¼ miles
		or
	27 July	King George VI and Queen Elizabeth Stakes, Ascot, 1½ miles
	20 August	Great Voltigeur Stakes, York, 1½ miles
	7 September	September Stakes, Kempton, 1 mile, 3f.
		or
	13 September	St Leger, Doncaster, 1¾ miles
	18 October	Champion Stakes, Newmarket, 1¼ miles

At four years	27 May	Brigadier Gerard Stakes, Sandown, 1¼ miles
		and/or
	7 June	Coronation Cup, Epsom, 1½ miles
	18 June	Prince of Wales's Stakes, Royal Ascot, 1¼ miles
		or
	21 June	Hardwicke Stakes, Royal Ascot, 1½ miles
	6 July	Eclipse Stakes, Sandown, 1¼ miles
		and/or
	27 July	King George VI and Queen Elizabeth Stakes, Ascot, 1½ miles
	15 September	Prix Foy, Longchamp, 11f.
	6 October	Arc de Triomphe, Longchamp, 12f.
	Totals	at 2 years 3/4 races
		at 3 years 5/6 races
		at 4 years 6/7 races
		Grand total 14/17 races

An important aspect to consider in planning a racing career is the reaction of the horse to the time of the year and the weather, which can cause his performance to vary greatly. Brigadier Gerard was a stone better in warm weather than he was in cold. Although he won both the Lockinge Stakes and the Westbury Stakes in the cold, he was unimpressive, but he was a different horse in the Prince of Wales's Stakes at Royal Ascot.

Conclusions

The breeding of racehorses is an inexact science. A good race-horse depends primarily on the genetic make-up, over which the breeder has no control beyond arranging a mating which might result in a desirable genetic pattern emerging.

The only guides available are the racing performances, characters and any other particulars concerning the sire and the dam. Intelligent interpretation of pedigrees can help, but only in terms of possibility, since no mating ever produces the same genetic pattern, however often it is repeated. Thus the genetic pattern of any foal and the resultant characters inherited by that foal are largely a matter of luck.

Nevertheless, some studs are consistently successful, while others do not produce results commensurate with the quality of their mares and the stallions used.

Given that the factor of luck in genetic inheritance does not discriminate between one stud and another, success or failure would seem to depend upon selection in breeding stock, arranging matings in which a desirable genetic pattern is most likely to emerge, and suitable environment, the latter embracing pasture, stud management, feeding, handling and, at a later stage, training, riding and race planning.

Investigation indicates that environment is a far more important factor than is generally appreciated. In particular, it entails suitable water and land, the latter not being over-horsed, properly farmed, grazed with bullocks and, by regular lifting of horse droppings, prevented from becoming horse-sick.

Sub-standard mares must be culled, whether they come from good families or not; and the breeder must be prepared for such culls sometimes to breed good horses in other hands. To avoid over-stocking his stud, a breeder may well have to dispose of good stock, but unless he is prepared to expand the enterprise this is inevitable.

The highest standards of racing performance, soundness, temperament, constitution, conformation and courage must be the breeder's aim, but since faults will have to be accepted, these must be weighed carefully against desirable qualities.

Trends in a stud must be watched carefully; if detrimental, every effort should be made to correct them before it is too late.

Above all, speed should never be lost.

Stock should be thoroughly tested on the racecourse, since only through the racecourse test can the true nature of a horse's merits and weaknesses be revealed. This information is of paramount importance to the breeder.

As in racing, there is only one thing that counts in the end: results. And if over a period of years results fall appreciably below reasonable expectations, something is wrong and the breeder must try to discover the cause: 'The fault, dear Brutus, is not in our stars, but in ourselves . . .'

Bibliography

Standard Works

Lehndorff, G., *Horse Breeding Recollections* (Horace Cox,
The Field, London, 1883).
> A short, but valuable and sound treatise written by a great
> authority on practical breeding.

Leicester, Sir Charles, Bt, *Bloodstock Breeding* (1st edition)
(Odhams Press, London, 1957).
> A carefully and intelligently written appreciation of all aspects of
> breeding. A sound, comprehensive and valuable work.

Sharpe, Harry, *The Practical Stud Groom* (2nd edition)
(British Bloodstock Agency, London, 1930).
> An admirable practical work by a first-class stud groom; a
> reliable guide.

Various, *Flat Racing*, The Lonsdale Library
(Seely Service, London, 1940).
> A review of all aspects of the subject by acknowledged experts;
> comprehensive, informative and generally sound.

Von Oettingen, B., *Horse Breeding in Theory and Practice*
(Sampson Low, Marston, London, 1909).
> A thorough, factual and informative work: one of the best books
> on the subject, written by an expert with wide practical
> experience.

Willett, Peter, *An Introduction to the Thoroughbred* (2nd edition)
(Stanley Paul, London, 1966).
> A concise and scholarly exposition of Thoroughbred breeding in
> general terms, lucidly presented. A helpful book for a newcomer
> to racehorse breeding.

General

Burrell, Sir Merrik, Bt, *Light Horses, Their Breeding and Management*
(National Horse Association of Great Britain, by permission of *The Field*, London, 1946).
 A clear, concise, lucid and practical pamphlet.

Craig, Dennis, *Horse-Racing Encyclopaedia* (J. A. Allen, London, 1963).
 A brief, scholarly synopsis of the function of racing and breeding. Especially recommended to new owners and breeders with no previous knowledge or experience of the Turf.

Hayes, Capt. M. Horace, *Points of the Horse* (Hurst and Blackett, London, 1907).
 A thoroughly researched treatise on the conformation, movement, breeds and evolution of the horse.

Hislop, John, *The Turf*, Britain in Pictures Series (Collins, London, 1958).
 A suitable book for bedside or lavatory.

Keylock, H. E., *The Mating of Thoroughbred Horses*
(British Bloodstock Agency, London, 1942).
 A useful little reference book to various theories and aspects of breeding. The interpretation is sound, but the author's conclusions on mating are more theoretical than practical.

Lesh, Donald, *A Treatise on Thoroughbred Selection*
(J. A. Allen, London and New York, 1978).
 A scientific study in trying to breed a top-class racehorse.

Llewellyn, Sir Rhys, Bt, *Breeding to Race*
(J. A. Allen, London, 1964).
 A concise, interesting study, written by a student of genetics with practical experience of breeding in various spheres.

McKay, W. S. Stewart, M.B., M.Ch., B.Sc., *Staying Power of the Racehorse*
(Hutchinson, London, 1937).
 An excellent book, of which the most interesting part is the author's views on stamina and the heart of the racehorse.

Milner, Mordaunt, *Thoroughbred Breeding, Notes and Comments*
(J. A. Allen, London, 1987).
 Views of different writers analysed and assessed.

Napier, Miles, *Thoroughbred Pedigrees Simplified*
(J. A. Allen, London, 1973).
    Pedigrees explained in relation to racing, breeding and sales.

Tesio, Frederico, *Breeding the Racehorse*
(J. A. Allen, London, 1958).
    A short dissertation on breeding racehorses, including some
    unorthodox and unscientific views. Any opinion of so
    distinguished a breeder as Tesio is of interest, but this is no guide
    to producing a Nearco or Ribot.

Ulbrich, Richard, *The Great Stallion Book*
(Libra Books, Hobart, Australia, 1986).
    An invaluable reference to 600 important stallions, from the
    earliest to modern times.

Varola, Franco, *Typology of the Racehorse*
(J. A. Allen, London, 1974).
    An international guide to the type of racehorse sired by stallions,
    based on personal research and dependent on updating.

Reference books published periodically

The General Stud Book (Weatherbys, Wellingborough).

Keylock's Dams of Winners (Keylock's Publications, Newmarket).

Racehorses of [1992, etc.] (annual) (Timeform, Portway Press,
Halifax).

Scrope, Alexandra, *Bend Or Graded and Group Winners* (*The Blood
Horse*, Kentucky).

The Stallion Book (annual) (Weatherbys, Wellingborough).

Statistical Record (annual) (Weatherbys, Wellingborough).

Genealogical

Bobinski and Zamoyski, *Family Tables of Racehorses* (J. A. Allen,
London, 1953); and Volume II, *1953–9*, updated by Toru Shirai
(Thoroughbred Pedigree Centre, Tokyo, 1990).

Jerdein, Charles, and Kaye, F. R., *British Bloodlines* (J. A. Allen, London, 1955).

Pryor, Peter, *The Classic Connection* (Cortney Publications, Luton, 1979).

Sharp, J. F. Mainwaring, *The Thoroughbred Mares Record* (Galopin Press, London, 1929).

Historical

Mortimer, Roger, *The Flat: Flat Racing in Britain Since 1939* (George Allen and Unwin, London, 1979).
  A comprehensive review of flat racing from 1939 to 1979.

Prior, C. M., *The Royal Studs of the Sixteenth and Seventeenth Centuries* (Horse and Hound Publications, London, 1935).
  This, and the following three titles, are the products of careful and reliable research.

Prior, C. M., *The History of the Racing Calendar and Stud Book* (Sporting Life, London, 1926).

Prior, C. M., *Early Records of the Thoroughbred Horse* (*The Sportsman*, London, 1924).

Prior, C. M. and F. M., *Stud Book Lore* (F. M. Prior, Bletchley, 1951).

Ridgeway, William, *The Origin and Influence of the Thoroughbred Horse* (Cambridge University Press, 1905).
  A scholarly study coming to an untenable conclusion.

Wentworth, Lady, *Thoroughbred Racing-Stock* (George Allen and Unwin, London, 1938).
  Colourful, entertaining, not altogether reliable and considerably biased towards the Arabian horse.

Breeding theories

Craig, Dennis, *Breeding Racehorses from Cluster Mares* (J. A. Allen, London, 1964).

Lowe, Bruce, *Breeding Racehorses by the Figure System* (Horace Cox, London, 1895).

Vuillier, Col. J., *Les Croisements rationnels dans la race pur sang* (Legoupy, Paris, 1902).

All the above contain some scientific flaw and, though of interest, should not be accepted as a whole.

Hewitt, Abram S., *Great Breeders and their Methods* (Thoroughbred Publisher, Lexington, 1982).
   A fascinating insight into the methods of some of the world's most successful breeders.

Veterinary

Hayes, Captain M. Horace, *Veterinary Notes for Horse Owners* (Hurst and Blackett, London, 1897; paperback edition Stanley Paul, 1987).

Miller, Wm C., *Practical Essentials in the Care and Management of Horses on Thoroughbred Studs* (Thoroughbred Breeders Association, London, 1972).

Rossdale, P. D., and Ricketts, S. W., *The Practice of Equine Stud Medicine* (Baillière Tindall, London, 1974).

Genetics

Jones, William E., *Genetics and Horse Breeding* (Lea and Febiger, Philadelphia, 1982).

Various, *Equine Genetics and Selection Procedures* (Research Publications, Dallas, 1978).

Some of the books mentioned above are out of print, but can usually be obtained second-hand from J. A. Allen & Co., 1 Lower Grosvenor Place, London SW1W OEL. They are the world's leading bookseller on equine subjects.

Index

Names of horses are in italic. Page references in bold refer to pedigrees.